A BRIEF
GRAMMAR OF
MODERN WRITTEN
ENGLISH

A Brief
Grammar of
Modern Written
English

ERNEST W. GRAY

The University of Toledo

THE WORLD PUBLISHING COMPANY

CLEVELAND AND NEW YORK

Library of Congress Catalog Card Number: 67–13626

First Printing

Printed in the United States of America

Published by The World Publishing Company
2231 West 110th Street, Cleveland, Ohio 44102

Published simultaneously in Canada by
Nelson, Foster & Scott Ltd.

Preface

The aim of this book is to present in a simple form some of the concepts of the "new grammar." It is intended to encourage the study of the language as an interesting pursuit requiring no practical purpose to make it a desirable activity. Yet, in addition, understanding the structure of the English language as presented in this exposition will give to those preparing for teaching English a tool that will make their presentation of language to pupils more lucid. It will also give to those interested in improving their writing a knowledge of the framework of the language within which all problems of style in writing must be solved.

It is intended also that an attitude of tolerance toward differences in dialects and in individual speech will be developed. To diminish the rigidity with which the study of grammar is presented in many classrooms is most desirable in order to reflect the changing nature and the tremendous flexibility of language.

Obviously the book owes a great deal to the students of linguistics over the past thirty years. The concepts developed by Bloomfield, Fries, Trager, Bloch, Smith, Gleason, Chomsky, Hill, Francis, Hockett and Roberts have been used continuously throughout the book as they must be by anyone writing about the language at present. However, the presentation of these concepts is, to the best of the author's knowledge, original, and the author is therefore responsible for any misconceptions of the ideas that may be found by linguists who may look at the book.

It must be emphasized that the book attempts to present a grammar of written English, that version of the language which appears in manuscripts and print designed to be read silently and which does not attempt to imitate the grammar of speech. This version of the language is practically uniform over the entire English-speaking area and thus is much more susceptible to a relatively simple display than is the spoken language.

As much as possible of the terminology of traditional grammar has been used in order to make the transition to the newer outlook on grammar less confusing to those readers brought up in the tradition. In some cases, however, new terms have been introduced because of what seems to the author their greater lucidity in naming the phenomena of grammar.

Throughout the book an attempt has been made to emphasize and illustrate the essential simplicity of the available structures of the language, while at the same time emphasizing the enormous possibilities for complications that lie in the possible combinations of these simple building blocks of the language. This seems to the author the great marvel of language, which makes it available to express the simplest concepts of the most unlettered people as well as the most sophisticated and subtle concepts of the learned. It is hoped that the book conveys this sense of the simple within the complicated and thus helps to create for the language the great respect and even awe that every student of language must feel as he investigates it.

I should like to acknowledge the help and encouragement received in writing the book from my colleagues in the Department of English at The University of Toledo, especially Professors William U. McDonald, Jan Solomon, R. L. Levy, Helen Cramer, and Mrs. Martha Manheim. Their criticisms arising from their use of the book in various classes have been of immense help. So too have the criticisms of students in my own classes, who have in the course of studying earlier versions of the book pointed out many flaws that I hope to have corrected, though, alas, no doubt many remain for which I bear the sole responsibility.

E. W. G.

February, 1967

Contents

A BRIEF
GRAMMAR OF
MODERN WRITTEN
ENGLISH

CHAPTER I

Introduction

Everyone who has attended school has been introduced to what teachers call "grammar." For most people this grammar has consisted of a good many definitions, such as "An adjective is a word that modifies a noun." Such definitions always turn out to have many exceptions, and these exceptions often cause arguments between students and teachers. Besides the definitions, rules are stated, ranging from "You mustn't use *ain't*" to "When a sentence has a compound subject joined by *and,* the verb is plural in form." The rules also have many exceptions and are often neither accepted nor obeyed by many speakers and writers. The study of these definitions and rules is by some teachers asserted to improve a student's speaking and writing. Others say such study is good discipline which trains the mind to be systematic and accurate. Many teachers assert that in order to understand grammar well one must study Latin. Still others assert that it is useless to study grammar formally, that it should be learned only insofar as the student needs it in order to make his speech and writing conform to the practices accepted by the teacher.

For many years there has been a great deal of controversy about the place of grammar in a person's education. Because there are so many attitudes toward the problem and so much uncertainty about its value, grammar has seldom been successfully presented, and most students feel that it is a dull, dreary process of memorizing or a useless waste of time, since they already have learned by trial and error to practice nearly all the specifications made by the rules.

The differences of opinion regarding the study of grammar result from a failure to think and wonder about language as a living, dynamic tool. Though it is easy to see that language is the device that makes men "time-binding"[1] beings (and therefore human), few have conceived of—and advocated the study of—language as a cultural or humanistic subject; language could be as valuable as chemistry and history in making us understand the nature of the world we live in. A moment's consideration will remind us that without first establishing some form of language we could have no chemistry or history or any other branch of learning. Language is one of the most essential tools for the establishment and sustaining of civilization; without it we should never have become truly human. Is it not strange that the study of this tool that makes us able to do all the civilized things that we human beings can do should be neglected, reduced to the learning of rules, and should in most educational programs simply be considered a chore or a service subject?

In this book the study of language will be taken seriously. It will be studied not because to study it is traditional or practical, but because a knowledge of language, especially of one's native language, is essential to being an educated person. Such study is essential because language is continuously fascinating in its capabilities of change and development, and because language now bulks larger than ever in the lives of all people on earth. Literacy—the ability to communicate and to receive communications in other ways than orally—is always one of the first concerns of a nation that is trying to impove the living standard of its people. In countries where nearly everyone is literate, the bombardment of spoken and written words is so steady and voluminous as sometimes to appall us.

WHAT LANGUAGE IS

Oddly enough the usual program of language study seldom makes any attempt to define language. For the purposes of this book *language will be defined as a group of sounds distinguishable from one another and arranged in a system by means of which thoughts and feelings (neural events)[2] can be communicated from one person to another.* Note that this definition does not include writing. The omission follows the practice of most modern students of language (linguists) in considering speech as the real language, writing simply a substitute for speech. (Hastily we should add that our intent is not to depreciate the importance of writing, which of course is the principal topic to be dealt with in this book; it is simply to point out the historical relation of speech and writing.) When it was realized that wisdom and knowledge could be passed from generation to generation only in limited amounts by speech, the human race was able to invent a substitute for the human voice, not equal in versatility it is true, but enormously valuable in preserving much knowledge that would otherwise have been lost.[3] Our libraries are the monuments to this invention. Writing has thus developed from speaking; it was, in its origin at least, dependent on speech, and even now speech seems to have a greater effect on writing than writing does on speech (except for the speech of very highly educated people whose contact with written language is much more frequent than is most people's)

The definition of language as a system of sounds applies to all of the nearly three thousand languages in the world—to English as much as to Japanese, to Turkish as much as to Ojibway. A single language, however, may be defined as a system of sounds familiar and usable to a limited number of people and unfamiliar to all others in the world. This means that the system has features that belong to it alone and that these features prevent the use of the system by anyone who has not learned it. Thus English has two sounds usually represented in writing by *th,* as in *this* or *thin,* which are not regularly present in the German or French language systems. This does not mean that German-speaking or French-speaking people cannot make these sounds. The physical apparatus used in making speech sounds is so similar in all human beings that everyone born without a physical defect can quite adequately make the sounds required by any language in the world. If a child of English-speaking parents had been kidnapped at birth and brought up by Turkish-speaking foster parents he would learn Turkish with the same ease as a child born of Turkish-speaking parents. In other words, language is a learned activity; there is nothing inherent about it. The great difficulty most of us have in learning a foreign language when we are grown is that through almost unlimited practice we have accustomed our muscles and nerves to make various sounds and to avoid others that have no place in our language system and would in fact simply be impediments to communication. Then when we try to make our muscles and nerves create unaccustomed sounds we encounter the resistance of habit. Any non-Britisher who has driven an automobile in the British Isles, where the rule is to keep to the left, will testify to the difficulty of responding properly to the necessities of such a traffic system. Even after weeks of practice a moment of relaxed attention will find one drifting toward the right. And in speech, so much more deep-seated in habit, the difficulty of learning unaccustomed sounds for many people is almost insuperable. Many Germans who learned their English as adults still, after thirty years of speaking English, say *zis* for *this,* and many Americans never quite learn to say the *r* in a French word so as not to make a native French-speaker grin.

A language then is a sound system known to and used by a limited number of people. It is obvious that some sound systems have many more resemblances than others. If we hear German spoken or Italian we are continually hearing what seem like English words rather badly mispronounced but still recognizable. When this occurs there are two possibilities. One is that the languages in question are related, that is, that they have a common ancestor or that one has developed from the other. The other possibility is that the people using the two languages have such similar cultures that they have borrowed sounds and other speech devices from each other. Though the first possibility is more likely, the second also exists, especially when a particular cultural activity has been developed in one country and then has been adopted by another. German and English sometimes sound alike because they are quite closely related. But sometimes Italian too, which is far more distantly related to English, sounds familiar. This is because certain cultural activities, music, for example, developed in Italian a vocabulary that has been taken over by English with little change. English is related to French, Swedish, Gaelic, Russian, as well as to German, though there is a closer relationship to German than to Russian or Gaelic. These languages and others are related because they have a common ancestor and they are said to belong to the same language family. English belongs to the language family generally called Indo-European.

Another word that must be defined is the word *dialect.* Everyone is aware that people who live in different parts of the United States speak a little differently. Eating lunch once in Ireland at the same table with four strangers, I thought I recognized the sound of one man's speech as that of someone from the southwest part of the United States, probably Texas. But the other three people didn't sound like Americans at all. And they didn't sound like Irish or English either. This was a bit puzzling. Later on I found that the first man was a Texan who had married a woman born in Ireland but who had lived most of her life in England. The other two were her relatives, whose history had been similar to hers. All of them spoke in a way that I could easily understand but in a way quite perceptibly different from my own way of speech. In other words they spoke different dialects from mine. *A dialect, then, is a version of a language having minor differences in the sound system which are clearly noticeable to a person speaking a different dialect of the same language, but which do not seriously interfere with communication.*

Dialects are not always connected with geography. Sometimes they are due to social differences. A man who has worked all his life as a laborer is not likely to speak very much like a minister or a judge even though each may have been born and lived all his life in the same city. Not only will the laborer's choice of words be different and more limited in range but the items in his sound system will not be quite the same. However, these men are not likely to have much difficulty in understanding each other, provided that they talk about subjects with which both are familiar. Many expert users of the language have at their command more than one social dialect, just as people trained for the stage often have these plus various regional dialects.

The written version of English is a sort of dialect, different from any speech dialect, yet an efficient means of communication among the users of widely varying speech dialects. It is of course not a dialect, strictly speaking, since it is not a sound system, but it has many resemblances to a dialect. Most speakers of English are thoroughly familiar with the "dialect" of written English.

And finally it is important to define a less familiar term, the term *idiolect. An idiolect is an individual way of speaking.* Each person has his own idiolect. It is because of this phenomenon that we can recognize the voice of an acquaintance even when we cannot see him —when talking on the telephone or from different rooms in the same building, for example. Nothing is more miraculous about language than the existence of idiolects. Every individual speaks in a recognizably different fashion from everyone else, yet this same individual with his unique way of speaking can (in the case of English at any rate) communicate successfully with literally millions of other people. No one speaks just exactly like anyone else, but over thousands of miles of the earth we speak enough alike to transfer our particular thoughts and feelings to one another.

The four terms—*language, a language, dialect, idiolect*—will occur throughout this book. You should understand them thoroughly; you must be aware of the existence in the world of the phenomena they name, and you must practice using the terms.

• EXERCISES

1. Look at a book written in Spanish, Italian, French, German, Swedish or Dutch and find twenty words that you think resemble English words. (Use a language unknown to you.) Write the English word of which you are reminded beside the word from the foreign language. Then by using an appropriate dictionary see if the word has about the same meaning in the foreign language as in English. Write the dictionary meaning of the foreign word in a third parallel list.

2. Listen to the speech of a person who belongs to a social group quite different from your own and try to describe the difference in speech apart from the choice of words. Write a brief report.

3. What do you think are the distinguishing features of your idiolect? Consider vocabulary, sound, speed, pitch or other items that seem important.

4. Compare the definitions of language found in several dictionaries and encyclopedias as prescribed by your instructor. What differences do you find? Write a brief theme (200–300 words) describing any differences you have found. Be sure to document your statements.

5. Describe in a theme your past experiences with what your teachers called grammar. In the theme answer such questions as: What did grammar consist of? How did your teachers seem to feel about it? How often during your years in school did the same things get repeated? Why were you studying it, according to your teachers and your textbooks? How did you feel about studying it?
6. If you have ever studied a foreign language, what did you find most difficult about it? Why? Prepare an oral report on this topic.

AN ATTITUDE TOWARD LANGUAGE

One of the great handicaps to the effective study of the English language has been an impression that somewhere there is a "correct" or "proper" English language, which should be the ideal toward which all users of the language should aspire. This impression is largely a product of the eighteenth century, when many scholars and writers felt that the English language was deteriorating and that unless strenuous efforts were made to save it, it would become so vague, ugly and distasteful that educated people would be unwilling to use it.[4] The "strenuous efforts" were made by writers of grammars and dictionaries who, being trained in the Latin language like all educated people of the time, were pretty generally convinced of the superiority of Latin to all contemporary languages. Therefore, to dignify English, they tried to demonstrate that it could be described in terms of Latin or, in other words, that Latin grammar and English grammar were practically identical and thus that English shared the dignity of Latin. The grammarians and lexicographers were aided by the fact that Latin and English are related, though rather distantly, and by the fact that many vocabulary items (words, prefixes and suffixes) show a distinct resemblance to the Latin language. For centuries Latin had been a sort of universal language, used by learned men in all the countries of Europe. Many terms, learned from Latin, passed into the English language, as well as into other European languages. It was tempting to those who noticed the resemblances between the vocabulary of Latin and that of English to assume that Latin and English were somehow closely related. Unfortunately for this assumption, the study of language has revealed that the occurrence of similar words in two languages is no real evidence of the close relationship of the languages. It seems that words are among the less important features of language. They can be picked up anywhere and if necessary invented. It is the *patterns* into which words fit that are the chief distinctive features of any language, as will appear later. It is clear, therefore, that a language like classical Latin and a language like eighteenth-century English might not be very closely related even though they had many words in common.

Let us take a very obvious example of unlikeness between Latin and English. In English if you want to say *Antony loved Cleopatra* you say it in this way and in this way only. To say *Cleopatra loved Antony* is to say something different. To say *Cleopatra Antony loved* or *Antony Cleopatra loved* or *Loved Antony Cleopatra* or *Loved Cleopatra Antony* is merely confusing and fails to communicate anything very certain. But in Latin it is possible to say all the following without interfering with the meaning of the sentence.

Antonius amabat Cleopatram
Cleopatram amabat Antonius
Cleopatram Antonius amabat
Antonius Cleopatram amabat
Amabat Antonius Cleopatram
Amabat Cleopatram Antonius

The difference between Latin and English is obvious; in English it makes a difference which word comes first, which second, which third. In Latin it doesn't make so much difference which order the words are in; the communication doesn't change or become vague. Thus one important difference between Latin and English is connected with the order of words. In English the order in which the words are put tells us something; in this example who loves whom. In Latin we are told this in a different way, by the *–us* at the end of *Antonius* and by the *–m* at the end of *Cleopatram*. The difference in ways of showing the relationship between words was disregarded by the eighteenth-century scholars when they tried to think of English in terms of Latin. So these scholars-turned-grammarians described an objective or accusative case in English that was distinguishable only by the word order. In Latin, with some exceptions, case involved a change in the form or shape of a word to indicate a change in its relationship to other words and had nothing particularly to do with word order. Thus case doesn't have the same meaning in English as in Latin, but nobody said this. Only six words in English have an objective case in the same sense that Latin words do. These are *I, he, she, we, they* and *who,* which would appear, if they were substituted for *Cleopatra* in the sentence *Antony loved Cleopatra,* as *me, him, her, us, them* and *whom.* All the other words in English can only be said to have an objective case as a result of their position, not their shape. If in our sentence we interchange *Antony* and *Cleopatra* we change their case, *Antony* becoming objective and *Cleopatra* becoming what *Antony* was, nominative. But only the position of the words has changed. So, while there is nothing wrong with saying that English words have an objective case, we should realize that this is nearly always a function of position, quite unlike Latin, where it is nearly always a function of shape. The confusion arises from using the word *case* to describe two different phenomena, and also from the creation of a case system based on Latin and including besides nominative, genitive and objective the dative case, which is a kind of ghost unless you think of it as a matter of word order.

The Latinized description of English, which was so awkwardly fastened to the living English language, established itself by becoming a part of the teaching of the schools. Unless this had happened, it probably would have been forgotten and later on, a description based on observation might have been made. But the eminence of Latin in the minds of school teachers, and the desire to avoid change, so common in schools, along with the tremendous growth in education through the nineteenth century has made this inaccurate and awkward account of the nature of English traditionally standard. Consequently most of us have been brought up to believe that learning the rules of this grammar and the terms which this grammar uses will make us speakers and writers of "good," "proper" English. Many people judge a person's speech and writing by how closely he comes to obeying the precepts of this system. However, the Latinate rules quite as often confuse us as help us. It is, then, as we see, the peculiar relationship to Latin that has created the notion—or more properly the illusion—of there being one and one only correct English. Since classical Latin is a dead language (that is, nobody now speaks it), it cannot change. Our traditional respect for Latin makes us want an English language that is also unchanging, though English, far from being no longer spoken, is used daily by more millions of people than any other language in the world, and, moreover, has changed continuously from the beginning of its history.

But of course deciding which of the many versions of English should be selected as the form to remain permanent is a rather difficult task for those people who want a standard, unchanging language. Perhaps it should be the language of our greatest author, Shakespeare. In fact, English is often identified as the language of Shakespeare. Well, take a look at some of the prose speeches in Shakespeare's plays, even the ones spoken by aristocratic and presumably educated persons, and decide how the "language of Shakespeare" would succeed today! Or perhaps we should settle for the "best" speech of the present time. Possibly the speech of the late President Kennedy, or that of the former Prime Minister of England, Mr. Macmillan, or that of the Chief Justice of the United States, Earl Warren, could serve as a standard. But one of these men spoke as a highly educated Bostonian; the second speaks as a very upper-class, highly educated Englishman; the third as a well-educated Californian. They all speak distinctly different dialects. Who would undertake to choose among them? Yet all three are successful speakers; all three are highly respected. Where can one find this elusive "correct" English?

There is, of course, only one answer: All of us must use a speech pattern that is acceptable to those people whose company we most value. If this means that we must learn more than one speech pattern we will do it, not perhaps consciously, but inevitably. Mr. Kennedy took his speech pattern from the prosperous, socially prominent group of people with whom he associated at home, at school and at the university. Since this group is not only the one in which he felt comfortable but also the one respected by many other people in this country, he had no reason to change it when he became a national figure. But if Mr. Kennedy had taken to the stage instead of to politics, he would without question have had to acquire a different manner of speaking, though he might not have forgotten how to use his native dialect. It is necessary to remember that language is a tool—a complex, fascinating and often recalcitrant tool it is true—that it is a device for accomplishing things. Its successful use must then be gauged not by the traditions of the grammarians and the schools, not by the snobbish prejudices of any self-appointed critics, but by its success in getting done what the user wants done. Nearly everyone through his own experiences almost instinctively recognizes this fact and there are few people who don't have the command of at least three dialects. One dialect is used at home in the circle of people whom you have known all your life, and also among your intimate friends. The second is generally a "work" dialect used on the job with people who have the same vocational interests. The third is a kind of formal dialect used with people of whom you must be careful because you can't predict what will be their response to your speech. The last is likely to be more "flat" and colorless than the other two, with fewer idiosyncrasies and short-cuts, a more conscious effort to select "good" words and, in the educated, a closer approximation to the standards of writing. Only the very ignorant and the very unsophisticated use a single dialect in all situations.[5]

As a result of considering these thoughts about correct English we must come to the conclusion that "correct" is practically a nonsense word when it is applied to English speech. The words "appropriate" and "effective" come far nearer to describing satisfactory speech than do "good" and "correct." Our attitude toward another person's speech should be an attitude of interest. We should be concerned to know why he speaks as he does, not to condemn him because he doesn't speak in the manner we expect him to. All of us have prejudices about speech; certain dialects and idiolects appear offensive to us in sound, in choice of words, in pitch, in loudness, in distinctness. We probably cannot avoid these prejudices, but we can certainly learn what they are and take precautions against their inducing us to make adverse judgments regarding people. Among my own prejudices (which are by no means unique) are those against high-pitched male voices, which seem to me effeminate; against the speech mannerisms of university-educated Englishmen, which seem affected; and against the "tough" dialect affected by many male adolescents who don't want to be thought sissies. My first response to such speech habits is to want to avoid the people who have them.

But yielding to prejudice sometimes deprives us of real benefits, as it would have done me if I had yielded to my prejudices against high-pitched male voices, for I should never have encountered in class and later made a friend of one of the very best teachers I have ever known. And I have found that people with the "Oxbridge drawl" are often lively and interesting and not affected at all. So if we persist in assuming that a person having a dialect we don't like can therefore have nothing important to say to us, we frequently cut ourselves off from interesting and valuable experiences.

• EXERCISES

1. Prepare to report orally on what you have learned to think about "correctness" in speech. How have you been taught to define or describe "correct English"? How have you responded to the definition?
2. Write a brief theme about a dialect of English that you dislike, making clear what features of it cause your dislike and what associations are involved.
3. If you were to choose a dialect other than your own to use publicly, what dialect would it be? Why would you choose this one?
4. You undoubtedly use a dialect at home with your family that is different from the one you use in English classrooms. After observing the differences for a week, describe in a 400-word theme the ways in which the two dialects differ. Vocabulary, idiom, pronunciation, sentences, should all be considered.
5. Select a 300-word passage of prose from a Shakespeare play. Rewrite it in what you consider modern English. Describe what changes you have made and why.

CHAPTER II

Phonemes and Their Written Counterparts

When anyone speaks he forces a column of air from his lungs through the oral cavity or the nasal cavity or both. This column of air may be changed in shape by changing the relative positions of the movable speech organs (tongue, lower jaw, lips). It may be stopped flowing, thus building up pressure, by closing the lips or even the glottis. It may be directed into the oral cavity or into the nasal cavity by the uvula. It may be caused to vibrate by tightening the vocal cords. All of these possibilities may be demonstrated by a little conscious manipulation.

If you open your mouth slightly and cause some air to flow out through the opening, a slight friction between the moving air and the oral cavity occurs. The slight sound that results is usually represented in writing by *h*, the first sound you hear in the word *hurry*. And of course if you hold your hand in front of your mouth you will feel the air column coming out of your mouth. Now if you consciously blow air through your nostrils, testing by putting your hand under the nostrils, you will no doubt find that your lips are closed. However, as you perform this exercise open your lips while still blowing air through your nostrils. You will find this easy to do, and if you hold your hand in front of your mouth you will not feel any air issuing. This exercise shows the effect of moving the uvula so as to close the opening either to the mouth or to the nose.

Next put your upper teeth lightly on your lower lip and again expel air from your lungs. The sound resulting from the friction caused by constricting the passage of the air and by changing the size of the oral cavity is that of the beginning of the word *fill*. Now place the front of your tongue against the bottom edge of your upper teeth and again force air from the lungs. The sound you get now is that which begins the word *think*.

Next press your lips together and try to push air through them. When the pressure becomes very evident, open your lips quickly. The puff of air coming through makes a sound like the one that begins the word *pet*. Now place the front of your tongue on the ridge just behind and above your upper teeth (the alveolar ridge) so as to prevent air from escaping through your lips. Force air from your lungs and release your tongue. The resulting sound is the one that begins the word *till*.

Making the sounds of English is essentially modifying in one way or another a column of air forced from the lungs. Of course many sounds that we can make are not used in language, though some are used now and then. For example, if you hit your thumb with a hammer you may make a sharp intake of air with the middle of your tongue against the roof of your mouth. This sound is not used in any English word. Or if you place your tongue against the bottom of your upper teeth so as to prevent the passage of air and then release it as the pressure of the air column increases, you will make a very definite sound, but one that English has not found any use for.

The combinations of those sounds that form actual English speech are characterized by other sound effects that contribute to successful communications. For example, one always pronounces a word with more than one syllable so that every syllable is louder or softer than the one which precedes or follows it. Such a word as *reveal* has a considerably greater force on the second syllable. If the force were reversed the word would not sound like an English word at all. This phenomenon is called "stress." Linguists generally agree that there are four levels of stress and that stress is an essential factor in determining meaning.

A sentence like *Where have you been?* pronounced in a normal fashion illustrates all four of the stress levels. The heaviest stress is on *been*. The next heaviest is on *where*. The third heaviest is on *you*, and the lightest is on *have*. Symbols to indicate the four levels have been agreed on. Applied to the sentence above they are: "Whêre hăve yòu beén?"[1] These denote relative—not absolute—stress. In other words, no matter how loudly the sentence is shouted the word *been* will receive a greater stress than *where,* and no matter how softly it is said, *have* will receive distinctly less stress than *been.* In fact, *have* may disappear if the whole sentence is lightly stressed; i.e., the sentence may be reduced to *Where yuh been?* But always the relation between the levels is preserved. In the last version the stress on *where* would still be greater than that on *yuh* and less than that on *been.*

The statements above show that stress exists and that there are probably four levels, but it does not show that stress is important in determining meaning. This may be demonstrated by thinking of the difference between such words as *cóntrast* and *contrást* or *próduce* and *prodúce.* Though the sounds are not exactly equivalent, the difference of stress is the essential determiner of meaning, since simply changing the sounds would not produce the meaning desired. One important feature of the English sound system, then, is stress.

Variations in stress are also used in speech to produce special effects. If the stresses are distributed as follows, a different effect from the normal is attained, e.g., *Whère have yóu bèen?* This might mean that the speaker is distinguishing *you* from some other person who also has been somewhere. If we mark the stresses in this way, *Whère háve you bèen?*, the effect conveyed by the speaker is that of anxious waiting. If we put them in this way, *Whére have yòu bêen?*, the speaker is perhaps making a correction, meaning "I said 'Where have you been' not 'How have you been.'" Stresses are therefore extremely important when we speak. The words alone cannot convey the variety of meaning possible without these subtle changes in the pattern of stresses. In writing you will notice that the meanings cannot be indicated by varying the stresses. For ordinary use certainly speech is a much more versatile tool than writing.

A second important feature in English speech is what is called "juncture." Juncture is what enables us to tell where the end of a word comes, where a unified group of words ends or where a sentence ends. It is not a simple matter like stress, but combines pause and a different treatment of the sounds coming immediately before the place of separation. Exactly which are the distinctive sound features of juncture is not completely understood, but the groups of phenomena that occur at certain points in oral discourse and that mark breaks in the even flow of sound can be quite well described and identified. The four most conspicuous occurrences are pitch changes, prolongation of sounds, fading and pause. Often these phenomena are accompanied by particular stress levels.

The most familiar juncture, the one easiest to identify, occurs most often when a speaker has finished a normal statement, that is, at the end of most sentences. In fact the occurrence of this type of juncture provides almost the only satisfactory definition of the term *sentence*. This juncture consists of a higher pitch at the beginning of the last stressed syllable followed by a lowering of the pitch and accompanied by a fading out of the voice and a prolongation of the last vowel in the sentence. After the fading, a perceptible pause follows before a second sentence begins. This juncture is called "double-cross" juncture, since the symbol # is used to mark it.

A second type of juncture, which also occurs at the ends of sentences, though much less frequently than the preceding, is the effect that occurs when we count slowly and deliberately or when we ask a question that requests confirmation of a previous statement. For example, if someone says *I want you to give me ten dollars,* and the person addressed says *Who, me?,* we have in the second sentence a good example of this type of final juncture. It is characterized by a rising pitch from beginning to end of the last syllable and a rather abrupt cut-off of the sound. It is followed by a distinct pause. This is called "double-bar" juncture from the symbol (‖) which is used to mark it.

The third type of juncture, which also occurs, but very infrequently, at the ends of sentences, can be illustrated by such an unfinished-sounding sentence as *Just as I was going over the——.* It more often occurs inside sentences. In the following sentence such a juncture would occur after the word *old.*

When I was eight years old, I moved with my family to Boston.

The chief feature of this juncture seems to be pause, accompanied by some prolongation of the preceding sounds. The pitch remains level. This is called "single-bar" juncture and is marked by the symbol |. It is sometimes quite difficult for untrained ears to hear a slight rise in pitch. Consequently, there will be some disagreement whether certain junctures are double bar or single bar. This is not important on the elementary level as long as the juncture is perceived. A peculiar feature of this juncture is that the manner of speaking seems to determine the frequency of its occurrence. A deliberate, rather formal manner of speech seems to show more examples of juncture than either the rapid casual give-and-take of normal conversation or the swift statements of, say, a radio or television newscaster or announcer. This phenomenon is probably due to the fact that the juncture is not easily audible in rapid speech, though probably detectable by a sufficiently sensitive recording instrument.

These three junctures may be called "final" junctures, since all of them *may* occur at the ends of sentences. In its appearance as a final juncture, each of them is associated with a mark of punctuation, # with the period, || with the question mark and | with the dash. It would be convenient if this relationship were invariable, but unfortunately it is not. Internally the comma frequently indicates a |, but also sometimes a ||, and not every | is marked by a comma.

The junctures also have a relation to stress. In English it is impossible to have more than one primary stress between any two examples of final juncture. Thus *I came, I saw, I conquered.* has three final junctures and three primary stresses. It may be marked *Í cáme* || *Í sáw* || *Í cónquered* #. A sentence such as *After we had finished dinner, we walked over to Joe's* might be marked *Àfter wè hàd fínished dinner,* | *wè wálked òver tò Jóe's* #. Final junctures and primary stresses go together. Of course the primary stress need not occur in the word immediately before the juncture. In the first sentence above, the stress might be *Í cáme, Í sáw, Í cónquered.*

A fourth type of juncture also exists. This is the juncture that marks the ends of words and is symbolized by a +. It is what enables us to distinguish between such things as *an aim* and *a name,* or between *lockup* and *lock up*. The principal feature of this kind of juncture is probably pause, accompanied sometimes by stress differences and also by prolonging the sound before the +. However, the pause is so slight that unless the speaker is very deliberate we are not very aware of it. All we can say is that something happens at the ends of words that doesn't happen inside words. But if we consciously slow down our speech we cannot help being aware of pause between words. Therefore if we say *The railroad right-of-way is overgrown* in a normal fashion we may not be aware of any especial difference between *right-of-way* and *is overgrown*. But if we slow down, we will notice a distinct pause in the latter combination that does not occur in the former.

In distinguishing between such combinations as *greenhouse* and *green house,* we have different stress patterns to aid our perception of the juncture, i.e., *gréenhòuse* as opposed to *grêen hóuse*. Of course we also have context, i.e., the words with which the combinations in question are associated. These often tell us what the speaker means, even if he uses an unusual pronunciation or does not say the word. For example:

> My father loved to raise flowers, even in the winter in New Hampshire. He tended his winter blooms like children. In fact he practically lived in his—— what do you call that place where they raise flowers?

Nobody is going to supply *grêen hóuse* to fill this gap.

The single-bar juncture (|) and the plus juncture (+) are often difficult to hear. Since people speak at varying rates of speed, with varying differences in pitch and stress, it is sometimes not possible for a group to agree on where junctures occur. But if the speech is made quite deliberate, the difference between these two junctures becomes apparent. For example:

> When it's over I'm going to go.

If this sentence is spoken quite rapidly there seems nothing different after *over* from what occurs after *it's*. But if we say it slowly and deliberately, we will notice a distinctly different effect at the two places. Also the combination *going to* may appear as *gonna* without a plus juncture. When said more deliberately, it generally appears as *goin' ta,* two words with a plus juncture between them. That is, the junctures are potentially present and presumably we recognize this potentiality even if we don't consciously hear it. When we don't recognize the potential juncture we are likely to fail to understand the speaker, whom we accuse of "running his words together."

It is quite obvious that stress and juncture exist only in connection with the units of sound that were mentioned at the beginning of this section. They, therefore, are phenomena that are imposed on the flow of sounds that form the basis of our speech. They are called "supra-segmental." It is our task now to identify and classify the basic sounds, the segmental phonemes of English.

• E X E R C I S E S

1. Mark the stresses in the following words: *bluebird, independent, retreating, silently, offhand, lighthouse, railroad, extraordinary, library, Detroit, cigarette, cement, introductory, manifest, overcome, chambermaid.*
2. Mark the stresses in the following groups of words: *auto dealer, babby buggy, instrument maker, the blue bird, a pretty girl.*
3. Mark the stresses in the following sentences as you would normally say them. Then by changing the stress pattern see what special effects you can get. When you arrive at a useful pattern for expressing a special meaning, explain what the special meaning is. (Do not change the sentences to questions.)

> I love you.
> We are working.
> I won the game.
> John cares for me.
> The result pleased Mother.

4. Mark the final junctures in the following sentences:

> I've got a headache.
> He came, didn't he?
> "After a while," he said impatiently.

5. Mark all the junctures you can hear when you say the following sentences aloud at a normal rate of speed. Then say each sentence

very slowly and deliberately to see if there are any potential junctures that you have missed. Re-copy the sentence with the potential junctures marked.

> After a while it began to rain.
> The sun shone and the birds sang.
> I'll be ready in a minute.
> The little boy on the tricycle just rode across our lawn.
> I know a man here who will help you.
> He died for love.
> He died for love had fled.
> Because of his speed he soon outdistanced the others.
> He soon outdistanced the others because he ran so fast.

6. Mark both junctures and stresses in the following sentences:

> My only brother, who lives near Boston, has been having
> trouble with his Rolls Royce.
> What kind of plan will succeed best?
> You have more than you need, haven't you?
> I'd like to have a few more, if you please.

7. Write a short theme that explains in your own words and with your own illustrations how stresses and junctures help to determine the meanings of sentences.

SEGMENTAL PHONEMES

First of all it is important to recognize that each individual speaks somewhat differently from each other individual, that is, each person has his own idiolect. This fact makes it possible for us to identify people by the sound of their voices. The separately distinguishable sounds that any individual makes in his speech are called "phones." We hear language only in terms of phones. When we listen to a person speaking we are hearing a series of phones that consist of individually identifiable sounds accompanied by other phones involving stress and pitch and prolongation and also by what may be

called "zero phones," or silences (pauses) between other phones. However, the study of phones, fascinating as it is, cannot by itself give
us any general knowledge of the language. What we must study is the
territory between the boundaries within which a phone must be
confined in order for one speaker of a language to communicate successfully with another speaker of the same language. For example,
let us take the sound we make when we place our lips together,
build up pressure behind our lips and then release this pressure by
opening our lips. If we were asked we would no doubt say that this
sound occurs in the words *pat, spell* and *stop.* If we hold a hand in
front of our mouth and say *Pat, spell, stop,* we will notice that the
p in *Pat* has a distinct puff of air following the release of the lips,
that the *p* in *spell* has no puff of air even though the lips are released
and that in *stop* the lips are not even released. Here obviously are
three different sounds. But do they make any difference in meaning?
We can easily test this by substituting in *stop* each of the other sounds.
A little practice will make this easy. And the result is negligible; no
one would think that anything except *stop* is being said. This shows
clearly that in English the three sounds are not distinguishable in
meaning, that is, the substitution of one of the sounds for another
does nothing to the meaning, though they may sound a little odd,
just as a distinctly high-pitched voice sounds a little odd without im-
pairing the speaker's capacity to communicate.

On the other hand, if we tense our vocal cords so that they vibrate and, after building up pressure behind the lips (as for *p*), sud-
denly release them we notice a change in meaning. *Pat* becomes *bat,*
spell becomes *sbell* and *stop* becomes *stob.* In other words we notice
that one word, *pat,* has become *bat,* while the other two have lost their
meaning, *spell* becoming a non-English combination, *sbell,* and *stop*
becoming a rare word, *stob.* That is to say, this change in the process
of producing the sound is perceptible and makes a very distinct change
in meaning. When change in the process of producing a sound results
in a meaning change, it produces what is called a different "phoneme."
A change that can be heard but does *not* change the meaning produces
a different "allophone."

Three terms that must be learned have now been introduced. To
redefine them:

(1) A *phone* is a separately identifiable sound made by an individual speaker.

(2) An *allophone* is a sound which is different from another sound but which does not cause a difference in meaning. Whether we use an aspirated *p,* a released *p* or an unreleased *p,* there is no real likelihood of misunderstanding. If we use them in the wrong place we may sound individually different, but not enough to make people misunderstand us. Such a difference is something like having a lisp or a particularly low-pitched voice. But if we use in a word a sound that seems to our listener to be different from one that he would use we run the risk of being misunderstood.

(3) A *phoneme* is all the allophones taken together, i.e., all the distinguishable sounds that can be substituted one for another without changing meaning. The three variants of *p* are all allophones of the phoneme /p/.[2] In other words a phoneme is a bundle of sounds that do not differ enough to pass outside a boundary that the language has set up. In a way the organization is like that of an American football field, where a number of things may be done—running, throwing, kicking—but all within the confines of a previously determined boundary. As soon as the activity takes players or ball beyond the boundary the game ceases to be the game called American football. Perhaps some other game is being played, for you can surely run and throw and kick the ball outside the boundaries of the field, but no longer can it be called American football. Thus in language, as soon as /p/ is voiced, i.e., changed to /b/, it ceases to be /p/. We have got outside the boundary of /p/ and within the boundary of /b/.

In another sense the word *phoneme* is a collective noun like *team* or *herd*. When we speak of a team, as in *baseball team,* we think of a unit, though all we can see is some individuals who differ widely from one another in physical as well as mental attributes. So the allophones in a phoneme may differ as do a shortstop and a catcher in a baseball team and yet be on the same team, the phoneme. *Phoneme* is simply a word by which we may talk about language in simple general terms just as *team* is a way of talking about a group who play baseball without naming each separate player.

Phonemes mean nothing by themselves unless they happen to coincide in sound with a morpheme[3] or a word. They are simply bundles of sounds that may be used in building a connected meaning-ful discourse. Like a pile of bricks they have nothing but potential significance until they have been organized according to a plan created in the mind of a human being. Phonemes include not only sounds like /p/ and /b/ but also the supra-segmental units, stress and juncture. There are, it is generally agreed, thirty-eight segmental pho-nemes (the ones like /p/ and /b/) plus the supra-segmental ones like ˆ or #, of which we use eight. There is considerable uncertainty about the exact number of supra-segmental phonemes. This uncer-tainty arises from our not being sure which of the phenomena that occur along with the segmental phonemes are meaningful. Further study will probably solve this problem.

Since there are thirty-eight segmental phonemes and only twenty-six letters in the alphabet, it is necessary to adopt special symbols to identify *some* of the phonemes. The phonemic alphabet has thirty-eight symbols, each one identifying a particular bundle of related sounds and nothing else. In this it differs from the ordinary alphabet, in which many of the symbols may stand for several quite different sounds, and the same or very closely related sounds (ones in the same phoneme) may be expressed by different letters. This makes the phonemic alphabet extremely useful, for material written in it can be read accurately by anyone who knows the alphabet; he has only to use the allophones he is accustomed to using in order to under-stand the meaning intended. Following is the phonemic alphabet, with words that for most American speakers will reveal the appro-priate sound.

Consonants

p	*p*at, s*p*ell, sto*p*, pe*pp*er	
b	*b*at, la*b*, a*b*le, a*b*out, *b*lind	
t	*t*rick, *t*ap, sa*t*, la*t*er	
d	*d*rink, *d*og, sa*d*, rea*d*er	PLOSIVES
k	*c*old, wa*k*e, *k*it, li*k*ing, a*cc*ount, *c*rime	
g	*g*un, a*g*ain, bi*g*, di*gg*er	

m	*m*an, so*m*e, su*mm*er	
n	*n*ot, ru*n*, a*n*y	NASALS
ŋ	si*ng*, si*n*k, bri*ng*ing	

f	*f*un, *f*right, stu*ff*, ci*ph*er, su*ff*er, rou*gh*	
v	*v*an, e*v*en, lo*v*e	
θ	*th*ink, smi*th*, e*th*er	
ð	*th*en, ei*th*er, brea*the*	FRICATIVES
s	*s*ink, pa*ss*, *s*pill, ki*ss*ing	
z	*z*inc, i*s*, ri*s*ing	
š	*s*ugar, por*ti*on, pu*sh*, *sh*ell, *Sch*ultz	
ž	a*z*ure, plea*s*ure, rou*ge*	

l	*l*ead, sea*l*, se*ll*er	LIQUIDS
r	t*r*ick, sto*r*y, *r*ight, hea*r*t	

č	*ch*urch, a*ch*ieve, ri*ch*, wit*ch*	AFFRICATES
ǰ	*j*erk, *judge*, led*g*er	

y	*y*acht, *y*es, law*y*er	
w	*w*ool, lo*w*er	SEMI-VOWELS
h	*h*ouse, re*h*earse	

Vowels

i	*see*, b*ee*t, b*ea*t, P*e*te, mach*i*ne, bel*ie*ve, s*ei*ze
ɪ	b*i*t, m*i*tt
e	r*a*te, sl*ay*, w*eigh*, br*ea*k
ɛ	m*e*t, r*e*gular, int*e*nt
æ	s*a*t, p*a*ss, c*a*n't, att*a*ch
ə	b*u*t, r*u*bber, *got*, r*ou*gh, *a*bove, r*e*peat, inst*a*nt
a	t*o*p, J*oh*n, n*o*t, f*a*ther
u	pr*oo*f, t*oo*, s*ue*, r*u*de, n*ew*, s*ui*t, r*ou*te (also with /aw/)
ʊ	p*u*t, f*oo*t, p*u*ll
o	b*oa*t, sl*ow*, d*ou*gh, th*ou*gh, n*o*te
ɔ	s*aw*, s*ou*ght

Diphthongs

ay	m*i*te, tr*y*, g*ey*ser, m*igh*t, l*ie*
aw	n*ow*, b*ou*t
ɔy	b*oy*, p*oi*se

The phonemic alphabet has three parts, as shown in the chart. The largest number of symbols is in the group called "consonants." These differ from "vowels" in their distribution; that is, they have different relations to each other and to vowels than do vowels to each other and to consonants. For our purposes, without trying to define too carefully, we may say that a syllable cannot exist without a vowel; it can exist without a consonant. In addition, a consonant sound interferes more with the air column from the lungs than a vowel sound does.

In attempting to learn these sounds and the symbols that go with them, it is absolutely essential to learn at least one word to illustrate each sound. (Note, though, that the sounds are different when said in isolation from when they are combined with other sounds in a word.) Thus it is necessary to learn three things, the sound, a word to illustrate its occurrence and the symbol to be used to represent it.

MAKING CONSONANT SOUNDS

A usual way of discussing the segmental phonemes is to describe the positions and movements of the various speech organs. This is called "articulatory phonemics" and can become very detailed. We will not attempt to describe all the details but will discuss the consonants group by group as they are labeled on pages 25 and 26.

You will have noticed that the consonants in the phonemic alphabet are grouped into plosives, nasals, fricatives, liquids, affricates and semi-vowels. We shall describe each group briefly, but first we must explain the terms "voiced" and "voiceless." If you will make a hissing sound (the phoneme /s/ as in the word *hiss*), and follow it with the phoneme /z/ as in the word *buzz,* you will have illustrated the difference between a voiceless and a voiced sound. Now make the two sounds in sequence as loudly as you can. Put a finger on the hard lump in the front of your throat. You will feel a conspicuous vibrating effect when you say /z/ that is not noticeable when you say /s/. You can also notice the difference if you put your hands over your ears and say the sounds. The /z/ is called a voiced sound, and the difference between it and /s/ is caused by the vibration of two membranes in your throat commonly called the vocal cords. When the vocal cords are relaxed the air passes through them without hindrance and we have a voiceless sound. When they are tightened the air pushing through makes them vibrate and we get a voiced sound. This difference is important in English; the phonemes may be divided on this basis. Of the thirty-eight sounds, the voiced ones include all the vowels and dipthongs, the semi-vowels, the liquids, the nasals and half of all the rest. This means that the plosives, the fricatives and the affricates are split into two groups, one group voiced, one voiceless; /p, t, k, θ, f, s, š, and č/ are voiceless, while /b, d, g, ð, v, z, ž, and ǰ/ are voiced. And the remarkable thing about the pairs in the groups is that voicing is the *only* difference between them. We arrange our vocal apparatus in the same way to say /s/ as to say /z/, as you must have noticed when you made the sounds. That this is important is seen when you realize that *pat* and *bat, but* and *bud, buck* and *bug* are only made to mean something different from each other by this phenomenon of voicing.

The plosives are sometimes called "stops." This term makes clear that the stream of air coming through the throat and mouth from the lungs is cut off at some point in the mouth and thus pressure builds up behind this position. The pressure is then released and the result is a mild explosion. The point at which the stopping of the breath stream takes place determines the quality of the sound; /p/ and /b/ stop it with the lips, /t/ and /d/ stop it by placing the tongue just behind and above the upper teeth, /k/ and /g/ stop it by placing the middle of the tongue against the middle of the roof of the mouth. The exact position of the tongue varies, of course, with individuals.

The nasals are made in the same way as the plosives, except that the air stream is permitted to go out through the nose; /m/ is made like /b/, /n/ like /d/, /ŋ/ like /g/. This is why, when your nose is stuffed up you can't say nasals very well and they come out like plosives. If you hold your nose so as to keep air from coming through it and try to say /m/ you will get no sound unless you release your lips. Then the sound will be /b/.

The fricatives are made by reducing the size of the opening through which the air stream passes so as to create friction and thus the characteristic rushing sound of those consonants. Like the plosives these sounds are made by placing tongue, lips and teeth in a particular relation to one another. For /f/ and /v/ one puts the upper teeth on the lower lip and the air comes out through the teeth. For /θ/ and /ð/ the tip of the tongue just barely touches the upper teeth. For /s/ and /z/ the front of the tongue almost touches the roof of the mouth just behind the upper teeth, and for /š/ and /ž/ the middle of the tongue just touches the middle of the roof of the mouth.

The liquids are made in a similar fashion, but the friction of the air stream is not so pronounced. The sound /l/ is made by touching the front of the tongue to the roof of the mouth and letting the air out along both sides of it. /r/ for most Americans is made by pulling the tongue back a little, and letting it touch the roof of the mouth somewhat farther back than for /l/ and then turning the tip of the tongue upward. However, a respectable /r/ can be made without turning up the tip of the tongue. There are also other ways of making /r/ used by speakers of other English dialects.

The remaining consonants, the affricates and the semi-vowels, are different from the preceding sounds because they require both a position and a movement. /č/ and /ǰ/ are made exactly alike except for voicing. As the sound starts, the tongue is touched to the roof of the mouth just behind the upper teeth as if to make a /t/. But as the pressure begins to build up, the tongue is quickly withdrawn and the air flows out with a rushing sound. So /č/ is half way between /t/ and /s/. When this sound is voiced it becomes /ǰ/.

The semi-vowels also involve movement, a rather pronounced movement for /w/ and /y/ and a slight one for /h/. If you say /w/ as at the beginning of *want* or *will,* you will feel your tongue moving back and up. On the contrary if you say /y/ as in *your* or *yes,* you will feel your tongue moving front and up. If you say /h/ as in *hurry,* the movement is less pronounced and occurs somewhere near the middle of the mouth. These sounds are very hard to say without their ending as a vowel, usually the vowel /ə/ (as in *but*). This is one reason for calling them semi-vowels. You will also notice that the sounds described above occur only before vowels. This enables us to use the same symbols /w/, /y/ and /h/ for the sound that follows an abnormally long vowel or as the second element in a diphthong. These sounds (/w/, /y/ and /h/) are called "off-glides" and have features in common with the semi-vowels.

One of the remarkable features of language is the economy with which the different sounds are made. Slight shifts in position and relatively few positions determine all the differences in meaning in our language.

MAKING VOWEL SOUNDS

All vowels are voiced sounds, and no vowel sound restricts the passage of the air stream as much as do consonants. The vowels are usually described in terms of the position of the tongue in relation to the roof of the mouth and its position in relation to the teeth. The vowel /i/, for example, as you can find out by saying the word *bee,* requires the tongue to be very close to the roof of the mouth and fairly well advanced toward the teeth. You can perceive this more clearly if you will say the words *bee, bath* and *boo* in succession, paying attention to the movements of your tongue. We will therefore describe each vowel with two words. The position in relation to the roof of the mouth will be described by the terms "high," "mid" and "low." The position in relation to the teeth will be described as "front," "central" and "back." /i/, therefore, is a "high, front vowel."

In addition to these two terms certain vowels require other descriptive terms. When you say *beet* and *bit* in succession you will no doubt notice that there is a sort of relaxed feeling in the second as contrasted to a tense feeling in the first. We shall therefore call some of the vowels "tense" and others "lax." And if you pronounce *beet* and *boot* in succession you will notice that in saying the first word your lips stretch out horizontally, while in saying the second they tend to purse up and make a roundish opening instead of the rather narrow slit required for making the vowel in *beet.* These vowels that require a rounded opening we will call "rounded."

We can represent the vowels listed on page 26 by a diagram, which is a simplified side view of the mouth.
This diagram relates the vowels to each other in regard to position as well as to tenseness and roundedness. It is also useful because it suggests that each vowel can move about considerably without getting into its neighbor's territory. Vowels are quite movable. In the history of English one can see that, while the consonants that have survived from Old English (O.E.) are pronounced very much as they always

i		u	
	ɪ		ʊ
e		ə	o
	ɛ		
æ			
		a	ɔ

have been, the vowels have often changed their sound completely. For example the word for *stone* in O.E. was pronounced /stan/; for modern English *ride* O.E. has /rid-/. Moreover, when one tries to write down in phonemic symbols what another person has said, there is usually no problem with consonants, but often it is difficult to decide which vowel phoneme best represents the sound. If several people listen to someone saying *I'll come in just a minute,* and try to hear what vowel appears in *just,* it is extremely unlikely that all will hear the same sound. The phoneme used to record the sound is likely to be /ɪ/ or /ə/ or /ɛ/. This variation may be due to inaccurate hearings, but it may be due also to a simple inability to decide which of these sounds is closest to the one heard. Looking at the diagram we notice that the territories of the three phonemes mentioned come together at one point. If the sound said in *just* represents that point, inability to decide which phoneme it belong to is inevitable. Consequently it is not to be expected that phonemic transcriptions of words by a number of people will always be the same even though they have heard the same sounds.

Considerable variation will also occur in what vowels people hear in unstressed syllables of words. Many unstressed syllables clearly have /ə/, as in /əbəv/ or /risənt/ or /ənkəvər/. But others are are not so clear. In *pity,* for example, some people hear /i/, in the last syllable, some people /ɪ/. In *install,* some people hear /ɪ/ in the first syllable, others /ə/. In *entice,* /ɪ/, /ɛ/ and /ə/ are heard. It is best not to quarrel about these deviations. As a matter of fact speakers probably differ in their pronunciations of the same word in accordance with the surrounding sounds and the speed and care of their utterance. We can say then that the vowels /ə/, /i/, /ɛ/ and /ɪ/ appear in unstressed syllables. Which one should be selected depends on what we hear in a particular utterance.

One other comment about unstressed syllables is necessary. In the speech of many Americans the consonants /l/, /r/, /m/, /n/ and /ŋ/ seem to by syllabic. *Little,* for example, sounds like /lɪtl/ or *written* like /rɪtn/. In order to keep the syllables in words distinct, such pronunciations will always be expressed with /ə/ in front of the consonant. This is an arbitrary rule, but it causes no trouble, since anyone reading our symbols will say them in the way to which he is accustomed. Thus *little* will always appear as /lɪtəl/ and *written* as /rɪtən/. And of course all other words with similar sounds will be similarly written.

Here then are the group of phonemes that are most likely to represent the basic sounds you need to communicate in English speech. And through written symbols for them you can use them in written communication. As long as we assign the sounds and the contrasts in sound we hear to the proper phonemes, we will be able to communicate successfully. When we do not recognize to which phoneme a certain sound belongs, however, we are in danger of having communication break down. We have various resources to use when we are worried about "getting" what someone says. (1) We may look puzzled if we are in the presence of the person who is talking to us. (2) We may be able to interpret the meaning from the context of the sound. (3) We may ask for a repetition or suggest the alternatives that occur to us. (4) We may be familiar enough with the dialect of our communicant to "translate" his phoneme into our phoneme. For example, if a person says what we hear as /hiy hæd tə klaym ə læder/ we are not likely to think the last word would be spelled *latter,* since the *climb* would rule out any such possibility. But if the statement goes like this: /ay hæd tə čuwz bətwinə læder/ ən ə rop, so ay tʊk ðə læder/ and if we can't distinguish any difference in sound between the last word and the seventh word, then there is no way to know whether he took the ladder or the rope. A person who says /havəd/ when he might say /harvard/ is not going to confuse us much because /havəd/ has no meaning in our dialect and because the context will prevent us from misunderstanding. But if this same person says /gɔd/ in a context where either *God* or *guard* would be possible we must look puzzled, ask or know his dialect so well that we understand that his distinction between *God* and *guard* is /gɔd/ and /gad/, not /gad/ and /gard/.

Even in American English, where dialectal differences are amazingly slight, we find these occasional confusions in speech, and we have to acquire enough linguistic sophistication to be aware of them and thus become able to deal with them.

• EXERCISES

1. Write the following words in phonemic symbols, with the stress placed as indicated: *cóntract, Detróit, éntrance, présent.* Then change the stress to the other syllable. Record what you think the new sounds are.
2. Write the following words as you would say them by themselves: *him, just, don't, my, can, have.* Now say aloud the following sentences in your normal manner of speaking and decide how you would represent phonemically the words listed above. Record the transcriptions of the whole sentence, including stress and juncture.

> We'll wait for him just a few minutes.
> They don't care for my reasons.
> You can have it; I have got one.

3. Write with phonemic symbols:

heart	bunk	luscious
can't	band	lawful
tribe	obey	clutch
black	antique	whinny
bleach	boyhood	whose
trace	trousers	weather
chum	thistle	whether
justice	singer	world
impeded	finger	leisure

vestige	wonder	Los Angeles
venture	rat	Miami
caution	rather	Mexico
passion	Wednesday	New Orleans
treasure	Detroit	Bangor
insane	Chicago	Virginia

Mark the stresses on all syllables in words of more than one syllable.

4. Write the following sentences using phonemic symbols for the segmental sounds and for the stresses and junctures.

I've looked for the judge everywhere.
That brash boy has been annoying my wife.
I don't like milk, do you?
Why don't you try a new diet?
He had a very severe seizure late last night.
I think it will be better, since he has no desire to go.

THE PROBLEM OF SPELLING

Spelling is of course the selecting of appropriate symbols (letters) to stand for the phonemes in our speech. By "appropriate" is meant those letters that will enable a reader to translate the written discourse into the same or corresponding phonemes in his speech dialect. Using the phonemes /gad/ as an example, how are we going to select from the alphabet we have learned the appropriate letters to represent successfully this particular sequence of sounds? For most Americans this is no problem; they would immediately select *God*. But people living in eastern Massachusetts, for instance, would just as unhesitatingly select *guard*. Which is the right way to spell /gad/? There is no "right" way, of course, and if the sequence of phonemes occurs in a sentence, we must rely on the context to give us a clue. The phonemes, in other words, have no prescribed or regular relations to the letters.

This is the cause of the spelling "problem." For not only do we have difficulty in selecting the appropriate letters for the phonemes used by a person who speaks a different dialect, we have also a problem of selecting appropriate letters to symbolize our own phonemes. The person who writes *taken for granite* when the written dialect demands *taken for granted,* or *would of* when writing requires *would have,* is suffering from the failure to know the written dialect well enough to symbolize his phonemes successfully. In the previous pages we have listed the phonemes of English, the bundles of sounds that, by their distribution, are the chief device for determining meaning. These phonemes we have identified both by a description of the physical procedure of making the sound and by a written symbol, each phoneme having its corresponding written sign. In the written dialect of English we cannot use these symbols: we have available only the alphabet and various marks of punctuation. The same alphabet and the same marks of punctuation are used throughout the English-speaking world. They are a unifying force, just as the uniform structure of syntactic units and sentences and the morphological changes in words are unifying forces. If we used a phonemic alphabet for writing, we should not have as much uniformity as we have now, for various geographical and social dialects would use various combinations of phoneme symbols to express similar brain events.

However, though the alphabet and other symbols used in the written dialect provide uniformity and thus facilitate communication, they also make problems. Translating phonemes of one's own spoken dialect into the symbols of the written dialect, an act which we call spelling, is one of the great educational problems today. People in authority demand "correct" spelling; thus much time is spent in school in attempting to teach children and young adults to spell. This task is discouraging both for teacher and learner—but in the present state of society it is necessary.

Essentially there is only one reason for spelling (i.e., symbolizing in terms of the written dialect the phonemes of one's own spoken dialect) and that is to provide successful written communication. If the symbols selected do this, there should be no reason for criticizing them, any more than a person who releases his /p/ at the end of a sentence is felt to be doing violence to the practices of the language. If a person writes *I would of come if I could of,* communication is not appreciably less successful than if he had written *I would have come if I could have.* Yet a person who habitually uses the symbol *of* to express what in the written dialect is normally expressed by *have* is looked on by many as horribly illiterate. Why? Presumably because it is bad manners not to symbolize in a way approved by such people as teachers, editors and other experts in the written dialect. As was said in an earlier chapter, many a man who speaks a dialect quite different from that spoken by most Americans is undistinguishable in his written symbolization. He has yielded to the pressure to be polite, just as we wear certain costumes on certain occasions, use various tools to eat various kinds of foods and perform certain rites in certain places. We find it pays to conform. We might feel quite honestly that it is a sign of inequality and therefore bad manners to rise when a woman enters the room, but it is impossible to explain our theoretical reasons on every occasion, so we swallow our convictions and get on our feet. Consequently the effective reason for learning to spell is so that we may promote convenience for ourselves and others by not doing odd things that require constant defense and explanation.

Anyone who wants to spell in his own peculiar fashion is welcome to do so, just as a person is welcome to try to dine at an exclusive hotel in dungarees and a sweat shirt if he is willing to defy the opinions of other people or to keep explaining his logical reasons for acting as he does. We learn to spell in order to add one more drop of oil to the wheels of society. It somehow does seem a waste to spend so many hours on such an essentially trivial matter, but there is no escape at present.

The reasons for the difficulty of English spelling are that the spelling of words has changed less than the sounds of the same words, that words which no longer contain certain sounds are spelled as if they did, that in borrowed words certain symbols have been retained from the original language and that some symbols have been inserted because of analogy or scholarly whim. Examples:

> *mite* used to have an /i/ but now has the diphthong /ay/ which is not reflected in the spelling. It also has a final symbol which used to be heard but is no longer.
>
> *knight,* which would phonemically appear now as /nayt/, has

symbols for two sounds that have disappeared (*k* and *gh*) and no symbol for one of the vowels that make up the diphthong /ay/.

pneumonia /numonyə/ has from the original language a symbol at the beginning which has never been said in English.

delight, spelled formerly *delite,* was changed because of the analogy of *light.*

debt, spelled formerly *dette,* had the *b* added as a recognition that it came from the Latin word *debitum.*

Add to these reasons the fact that spelling reflects dialect differences in the Middle Ages and various spelling reforms that partly were accepted by language users and partly not, and the confusion is understandable.

As a result most of the phonemes are represented in the written dialect by a variety of written symbols and most of the written symbols may stand for more than one phoneme. Here are some examples:

/p/   ha*pp*y, ho*p*e
/b/   *bubb*le
/t/   *tat*ter, *phth*isic, *Th*omas, *t*alked
/d/   *dodd*er
/k/   *k*ind, *c*at, te*ch*nical, de*ck*, De*kk*er (proper name), *q*ui*ck*
/g/   *g*et, da*gg*er, *gh*ost
/f/   *f*ew, *ph*one, di*ff*er, rou*gh*
/v/   *v*ery, o*f*
/θ/   *th*in
/ð/   *th*is
/s/   *s*it, *sc*issors, mi*ss*
/z/   *z*est, i*s*, di*zz*y, sci*ss*ors
/š/   *sh*oot, *s*ugar, pa*ss*ion, cau*t*ion, *ch*ute
/ž/   a*z*ure, plea*s*ure, ver*s*ion, gara*g*e (in some dialects)
/č/   *ch*ur*ch*, pas*t*ure
/ǰ/   *j*ust, gru*dg*e, *g*erm, re*g*ion
/m/   *m*an, *m*u*mm*y, plu*mb*
/n/   *n*ut, *n*i*nn*y

/ŋ/   thi*ng*, si*n*k
/l/   *l*ot, i*ll*ustrate, litt*l*e
/r/   *r*un, e*rr*or
/w/   *w*on, *wh*ere (in many dialects)
/y/   *y*et
/h/   *h*igh, w*h*o

All vowels with minimum stress are likely to belong to the phonemes /ə/ or /ɪ/, though there are individual differences of course. The following examples refer only to vowels in syllables bearing primary, secondary or tertiary stress.

/i/   m*ee*t, m*ea*t, repr*ie*ve, pr*e*c*e*de, Ph*oe*bus, k*ey*
/ɪ/   b*i*t, *i*nvent, j*u*st
/e/   br*ai*n, b*ay*, g*au*ge, th*ey*, st*ea*k, *ei*ght, s*a*ne, G*ae*lic
/ɛ/   b*u*ry, s*ai*d, m*a*ny, ag*ai*n, cr*e*dit, s*ay*s, br*ea*th, h*ei*fer, l*e*opard
/æ/   gl*a*d, g*ua*rantee
/ə/   *a*bove, bl*oo*d, c*ou*ple, st*u*ff
/a/   p*a*lm, s*e*rgeant, h*ea*rth, J*oh*n, f*o*g, ps*a*lm
/u/   b*oo*st, d*o*, br*ui*se, cr*u*de, v*ie*w, sh*oe*, rh*eu*matic, n*ew*, y*ou*, *ewe*
/ʊ/   b*oo*k, p*u*ll, w*ou*ld, b*o*som
/o/   cr*ow*, t*oe*, s*ew*, g*o*ld, c*oa*rse, d*oo*r
/ɔ/   *ou*ght, *au*dible, w*a*r, cl*o*th, y*aw*n

Diphthongs

/ay/   appl*y*, appl*ie*d, l*y*e, *ai*sle, h*ei*ght, wr*i*te, b*uy*, wh*y*, ch*oi*r
/aw/   c*ou*nty, s*au*erkraut, d*ow*n
/ɔy/   b*oy*, *oi*l

These are examples of the difficulties that arise when we try to represent certain phonemes by the symbols of the written dialect.

The result of all this is that to an ordinary user of English there is no rhyme nor reason in the relationship between the sounds he says and the letters he writes. Each word, it seems, must be learned in itself, since the principle of analogy, by which we unthinkingly and correctly add –*s* or –*es* to a new word we want to pluralize, doesn't seem to work with any consistency. Of course each word that appears irregular can have its spelling accounted for by studying the history of the word. But this is a very slight consolation to a college freshman whose instructor has been belaboring his poor spelling. Analogy *does* work in many cases, and logical spelling rules are not unknown. A desire to learn the "good manners" of the written dialect so as not to offend its users is the chief weapon at the command of the uncertain speller. Of course in rare instances there are people with psychological quirks, who can be helped only by psychological treatment. But most poor spellers are poor spellers because they never cared about being anything better. The most successful motive for becoming a better speller is to want to belong to the group that spells correctly.

- **EXERCISES**

1. Write phonemically: *though, through, plough, rough.* Look the words up in *The New English Dictionary* and find out why the last four letters differ in pronunciation while remaining the same in spelling.
2. How do you account for such spellings as *of* for *have, taken for granite* for *taken for granted, whether* for *weather, were* for *where, folksail* for *forecastle*? Use phonemic symbols to explain the spelling of *prehaps* for *perhaps, smokey* for *smoky, inheritence* for *inheritance, vengence* for *vengeance, enhants* for *enhance, studing* for *studying, dinning* for *dining.* Expand your explanation into a unified theme with a beginning and a conclusion.
3. How would you spell the following nonsense words: /rečkəm/, /prɛšɪlet/, /jɔmɪlot/, /aydəč ut/, /dətrɔymas/ , prɪlənt/, /pangoθimet/, /brutɛlɪkəm/, /yɛðmət/, /mɪtəlpuškan/?
4. Write a brief essay on your own spelling problems, if you have any. Explain as best you can the types of words that you misspell and, on the basis of this chapter, account for the difficulties. If you have no spelling problem, write briefly on how you learned to spell accurately and offer some suggestions to bad spellers.

CHAPTER III

Morphemes and Words

Phonemes and letters have no meaning in themselves except by the accident of coinciding with one of the meaningful units of language. The word *a,* written phonemically /ə/, is an example of such a coincidence. Usually it is only by combining or by having a particular relationship with other phonemes or letters that phonemes acquire meaning. The fundamental unit of meaning is called by linguists a "morpheme." Morphemes often coincide in shape with words, but morphemes are not by any means always words. They are, in effect, units that have meaning in themselves, whether or not they can be written as words in sentences. Any ordinary dictionary lists a great many morphemes that do not coincide with spoken or written words. For example in *Webster's New World Dictionary** is the following:

> **-er** (ẽr), a suffix of various origins, functions, and meanings: 1. [ME. *-er(e);* AS. *-ere;* WGmc. **-arj,* **-ārj;* reinforced by L. *-arius, -arium,* agentive suffixes, (Anglo-Fr. *-er, -ier*), L. *-arem* (OFr. *-er*), L. *-aturam* (OFr. *-ẽure*), L. *-atorium* (OFr. *-ẽor,* Fr. *-oir*), L. *-atorem* (OFr. *-ẽor*)], *a*) added to nouns, meaning *a person having to do with,* as in *hatter, cottager:* also **-ier** or **-yer** after *-w* and in a few words with Anglo-French *-ier,* as in *lawyer, hosier. b*) added to place names, meaning *a person living in,* as in *New Yorker. c*) in colloquial usage, added to nouns, noun compounds, and noun phrases, meaning *a thing or action connected with,* as in *diner, double-header. d*) added to verbs, meaning *a person or thing that,* as in *sprayer, roller;* see also **-ar, -or.** 2. [ME. *-re, -er;* AS. *-ra*], added to many adjectives and adverbs to form the comparative degree, as in *later, greater.* 3. [ME.; Anglo-Fr. inf. suffix], added to verb bases in legal language, meaning *the action of* ——*ing,* as in *demurrer, waiver.* 4. [ME. *-ren, -rien;* AS. *-rian,* freq. suffix], added to verbs and verb bases, meaning *repeatedly,* as in *flicker, patter.*

* *Webster's New World Dictionary of The American Language,* College Edition, © 1966 by The World Publishing Company, Cleveland, Ohio.

This little two-letter or two-phoneme combination, which when written by itself is preceded by a one-en dash (this is important), never appears alone in actual speech or writing, but in combination it has an extensive application in English. *–er* is called a "bound" morpheme, because it does not normally appear without being attached to some other combination of phonemes. This bound quality is signified by the preceding dash. We may say that the dash is, so to speak, a morpheme in the written dialect, since putting it in front of or behind a combination of letters adds to the meaning of the combination "is to be attached to something else." There is no such morpheme, of course, in the spoken language.

In addition to bound morphemes there are also "free" morphemes. Free morphemes can be written by themselves and are equivalent to words. The word *wholesale* is made up of two free morphemes, *whole* and *sale*. The word *return* is made up of a bound morpheme, *re–*, followed by a free morpheme, *turn*. The word *prevail* is made up of a bound morpheme *pre–*, followed by a second bound morpheme *–vail*.

The word *morpheme* like the word *phoneme* stands not for a single unit, but for a group or bundle of units. This may be illustrated by the fact that the morpheme in English which means "more than one" does not always have the same shape. If we add to the word *rat* the morpheme meaning more than one it sounds /s/ and looks *s*. If we do the same for the word *rod* the morpheme sounds /z/, though it is still written *s*. If we add the morpheme to *box,* it sounds /əz/ and is written *es*. That these three forms are related seems rather obvious from their sound and appearance, and all have precisely the same meaning. We say then that in English the morpheme meaning "more than one" appears in one of three allomorphs when spoken and in one of two allomorphs when written. These three (two) allomorphs are in contrast, that is to say we cannot use any one of the three at will; we must use the one that belongs in the context. So when a word ends with /s/, /z/, /š/, /ž/, /č/, or /ǰ/ we *must* use /əz/. But if the word ends in any other unvoiced sound we cannot use /əz/ but must use /s/. If it ends in a voiced sound other than /z/, /ž/ or /ǰ/ we *must* use /z/ and never either of the others.[1]

The study of morphemes is called "morphemics," and a special branch of morphemics is the study of the changes of shape in a base form[2] of a word that produce changes in the meaning of a word. This branch of morphemics is called "morphology," and the various morphemes added to the words are called the "inflections" of the word. Most college students have devoted a great deal of time to the study of inflections, or, more accurately, to the study of the "correct" way to *use* the various inflections.

For example, most of us are aware that *he, his* and *him* are varying forms of the same word, and that they cannot be interchanged at will. We can write

He is walking down the street.

but we cannot in any normal written dialect I have encountered write

Him is walking down the street.

We can possibly write

His is walking down the street.

but only under special circumstances.

Morphology is the study of how the varied forms of a word are distributed in the language. And of course the morphology of the written dialect is the study of normal distribution in this dialect. An illustration of a distribution problem in the written dialect is

It is not possible to buy these kind in England.

The distribution of *these* in front of a non-plural noun is abnormal in the written dialect. So we must point out that the normal form for the written dialect, whatever it may be in the spoken dialect of the writer, is *this.*

It is not possible to buy this kind in England.

Problems that relate to the distribution of forms and structures in particular dialects are called "usage problems." They must be kept apart from grammatical problems. Grammar is concerned with all the distributions that any dialect has found useful in successful communication, and therefore grammarians are just as much interested in the baby-talk

Me wants candy.

or the vulgar

I ain't never seen no such house.

as they are in the language of the mature, educated user of English.

Usage, on the other hand, is concerned with what is appropriate in a certain dialect. The student of usage might find *Me wants candy* good enough and rather cute for a two-year-old child, but would certainly find it inappropriate for a high-school student, in either speech or writing. One must first define the appropriate environment for various dialects before deciding what is proper for a particular dialect such as the written dialect. Many highly educated people whose spoken and written usages are much alike find it difficult to accept the fact that appropriateness is the test for usage. They find it easier to condemn a usage as wrong because it does not agree with their usage than to take the trouble to consider whether or not the usage in question is appropriate. It is always more accurate to say that a particular usage that one dislikes is inappropriate to one's own spoken dialect than to condemn it completely. And even in written English one can't be sure that he is "right." For example, in England it is appropriate to say *The government have proposed a bill,* whereas in the United States one would say *The government has proposed a bill.* We cannot say either is wrong. Each is appropriate in its place.

The difference between a grammatical problem and a usage problem may be illustrated by the two sentences below.

He most of all wanted a good meal and a drink wouldn't do.

presents a grammatical problem, because the absence of any indication that *and* does not connect *meal* and *drink* interferes with successful communication and violates a basic principle of English structure. On the other hand the sentence

He asked who Joe had invited to go swimming.

presents a usage problem, because only in the written dialect or in the speech of very few people would *whom* be appropriate instead of *who*.

It is extremely important to keep this difference continuously in mind, for most people usually say something is wrong when it differs in usage from the dialect that they use or admire.

We shall continue our study of inflections when we discuss the chief syntactical devices of English grammar.

It is not always easy to be sure how many morphemes are contained in a particular word. We usually begin by comparing the given word to others that contain the same written form or the same sound combination. We are, for example, used to seeing the bound morpheme *–ness* at the ends of words. We notice it in *kindness, happiness, smallness, skillfulness, promptness* and many others. We also notice that when we remove the *–ness* from these words, a combination is left that is a free morpheme in English. So we have no problem in recognizing this *–ness* as a morpheme and in identifying its meaning. But when we run into words like *income, inlet, incompetent, incomplete,* we shall be in trouble if we think *in* has the same meaning for all these words. For in the first two it has to do with direction and is thus an example of the free morpheme *in,* while in the second pair it means *not* and is an example of the bound morpheme *in–.* Therefore, because of this difference in meaning we must suppose that there are two morphemes, one spelled *in,* the other *in–,* just as there are two free morphemes spelled *bear.* This is one difficulty in assigning combinations of letters or sounds to a morpheme.

Another difficulty arises from the extensive borrowings made by English from other languages, especially from Latin and French. If we don't know those other languages, we have great difficulty in identifying the bound as well as the free morphemes. However, common sense helps somewhat. If we have a series of words such as *calamity, charity, capacity, sanity,* we might well guess that *–ity* was a morpheme—either bound or free—and that there were at least two morphemes in these words. In actual practice, of course, no one who didn't know Latin or who didn't have access to a good etymological dictionary could go any farther than that. Whether *calam–*, *capac–* or *reciproc–* is a single morpheme or more than one would be impossible to tell from English alone, though, because of the great number of words beginning with *re–*, one might guess that *reciprocity* had at least three morphemes.

In English then, being able to identify morphemes requires not only comparison of form and meaning, but also knowledge of foreign languages. For a person unfamiliar with foreign languages a dictionary with as complete etymologies as possible must be used in discovering the separate morphemes of a word.

Besides the morphemes that are coincident with or composed of segmental phonemes, there are others that involve supra-segmental phonemes. These we shall simply illustrate, merely pointing out an obvious example or two, at the same time emphasizing that the complications in dealing with these phenomena are enormous and by no means wholly understood.

In speaking, the juncture # usually means "end of sentence," and the juncture ‖ means "end of particular kind of question or a deliberate, thoughtful listing of items." Just so in writing, the symbols for these junctures mean something. A period means the end of a sentence that is not a question. A question mark means a question sentence when there is no other evidence. An exclamation mark means a certain distribution of stresses and pitches that gives the exclamatory effect to the sentence. The various combinations of pitch, stress, pause, speed, etc., that determine so much of meaning in speech and that have not as yet been completely analyzed have no symbolization in written English, and therefore must be suggested by descriptive words. In the writing of novelists this technique can be seen in action. Here are some examples, taken from Chapter XVII of Conrad's *Lord Jim*. Notice that in actual speaking, the words describing the manner of speech would be unnecessary because of supra-segmental morphemes. These words are italicized.

(1) "I suppose you intend to eat and drink and to sleep under shelter in the usual way," I remember saying *with irritation.*
(2) "You can't," he said *very simply and gently.*

(3) "But I can," I *insisted*.

(4) "Upon my word you deserve being told to go to the devil," I *cried, forcing the note of indignation.*

(5) "Jove!" he *gasped out.*

(6) "And I have never seen," he *shouted.*

(7) "You have given me confidence," he *declared.*

By the use of descriptive words written language tries to make up for its lack of adequate symbols for supra-segmental morphemes.

WORDS

Up to this point we have been using the term *word* as if it were perfectly clear what was meant by it. It is like many widely used and common terms, difficult if not quite impossible to define. When we are reading a printed page we seem to identify words by the fact that there is a wider space around certain groups of letters than there is before and after the letters that compose the group. This is no doubt an interesting observation, but if we are doing the writing, our problem is where to leave these larger spaces. We must decide whether to write *high school teacher* or *high-school teacher* or *highschool teacher*. And we cannot avoid this sort of decision if we are going to write at all. How do we know which to write? I suspect that most people resort to oral practice, that is, they say the sounds to themselves and on the basis of the sounds decide how to write it. So we go back to spoken language to guide us in writing.

One practical and relatively easy way to determine whether a certain form is a word or not is stated by Charles F. Hockett in his book *A Course in Modern Linguistics.**

So as the first step in determining the words in an utterance, we ask speakers to repeat the utterance slowly and carefully. Suppose someone has just said *John treats his older sisters very nicely* in the normal rapid way. . . . If we ask for a slow repetition, he may break the sentence up into as many as seven suc-

---

* Charles F. Hockett, *A Course in Modern Linguistics* (New York: The Macmillan Company, 1958) pp. 166–167.

cessive units, each with its own intonation and with intervening pauses: *John, treats, his, older, sisters, very, nicely.* Or he may not pause quite so often: *his older,* or *very nicely,* might be kept as a single unit. Thus we may have to elicit more than one slow careful delivery before we can be sure we have obtained the maximum break-up. Only under very artificial conditions, however, would anyone pause at additional points, say between *old* and *–er.*

A word is thus any segment of a sentence bounded by successive points *at which pausing is possible.* The example contains seven words. It contains this number whether actually delivered as one unit or as several, since words are defined in terms of *potential* pauses, not the actual pauses in any one delivery.

Our success in using the method described by Mr. Hockett is dependent on our informant. If we are our own informant, we can be successful only insofar as our dialect coincides with that of our possible critics. For example, if we try to slow down our saying of *I'm not gonna do it* and our dialect doesn't recognize the possibility of *gonna* becoming *going to,* we shall be unable to meet the requirements of the written dialect in ending these two words at the "right" places. It seems unlikely, though, that this particular situation would arise among students who have progressed beyond high school.

Perhaps the best way to appreciate the efficacy of Mr. Hockett's method is to try to slow down the saying of the following pair of contrasting sentences and watch what happens to the form *greenhouse* as compared to the forms *green house.*

We saw the flowers in the green house over there.
We saw the flowers in the greenhouse over there.

No matter how slowly and deliberately we say the second sentence, there is never a pause between *green* and *house* as there is in the first sentence. So ultimately the test for a word in speech is much like the test in writing, i.e., it is bounded by larger spaces than those that occur within the boundaries.

• EXERCISES

1. Open a desk dictionary at random and list all the morphemes you can identify from one column of a page. Write a brief explanation of how you decided that the forms you selected were really morphemes. Make a separate list of those words that contain possible morphemes that you are not sure of. Classify the morphemes you have found as bound or free.

2. How many morphemes does each of the following words contain: *obscured, breadth, undercoating, cylinder, unfaithfulness, parenthood, perhaps, decides, machinery, misjudgment?* Classify each one as bound or free and give its meaning.

3. How many words do you think are in each of the following sentences?

/may brəðərz gənə gɛt ə nuw steyšən wægən ənə yɔt/
/wəts ə lil kwarl əməŋ frenz/
/aydə now wəčə takn əbawt/
/ðərz owni ə lɪl bɪt əv ɪt lɛft/

WHAT IS A SENTENCE?

Sentences used in speaking are considerably different from sentences used in writing, not only because written sentences can only be seen and not heard, but also because of the way in which they are constructed. It is rather easy to see why this is so. When we talk with people, there is always an alternation of speakers. Only when making a speech does a speaker continue from his first word to his last without stopping, and often in this situation he is reading or repeating from memory what he has previously written down. He really isn't speaking; he is making speech sounds out of written symbols. But in really spontaneous speech there is seldom a single speaker. Nearly every time any speaker except the first one starts to speak he is responding to something a previous speaker has said. As a result a good many words need not be repeated. If you meet an acquaintance on the street and ask him, *Where are you off to now?* he may say *I'm going home,* but he is just as likely to say simply, *Home.* And the word *home* is a sentence. We know it is a sentence because the final juncture is what it is. It is marked off as a unit by the fact that he began to speak after you had stopped and by the fact that he made suitable sounds as his speech came to an end.

A sentence, then, may consist of a single morpheme or a single word. Also a sentence may consist of a group of several words. On a miserable, snowy, windy day some athletic friend might say, *Let's walk home.* And your response might quite likely be *In this weather?* However, not just any combinations of words can form sentences in speech. The combinations are limited in number and can be recognized by their shape as well as by the final juncture. For instance, it would be quite impossible to think of a situation in which a sentence consisting of the words *In the.* would be appropriate; but the combination *In the morning.* is quite natural in sound and would often be appropriate.

Not any casual combination of words can normally be used in speech as a sentence. We can use only a few structures that we learn to make early in life without consciously knowing that we are learning to make them. As a result of this limitation, these few normal ways of grouping words can be identified and listed and thus show us the forms into which words can be fitted to make successful units of communication.

As the first step in determining what these combinations of words are, let use list some speeches that are beginning speeches, i.e., that do not require that a previous bit of speech has occurred, and some appropriate responses to them. This will give some idea of the variety of shapes that can make sentences. We will start with some single word responses.

1. Are you for or against Westerns?
   Against.
2. Do you like love or money better?
   Money.
3. Do you like red or white roses better?
   Red.
4. How did the play start?
   Slowly.
5. When you last saw John, what was he doing?
   Practicing.

And now we will list some word combinations.

1. What's the importance of driving lessons?
   To teach safety.
2. Where've you been?
   At the library.
3. What have you decided about Roger?
   That he must be put on probation.

4. Do you still like Bach?
   More and more.
5. What size should you like?
   A small one.
6. What do you know about Abraham Lincoln?
   He freed the slaves.[1]

It will be noticed that only the last of these answers has a form that would suit most of the usual definitions of the term *sentence*. This would be called a sentence because "It has a subject and a predicate" or "It expresses a complete thought." These are the two most popular definitions for sentences. What they mean is hard to say. In fact we accept them wholly because we have come to know that if we call a word group that looks like *He freed the slaves* a sentence, we will be making a "correct" answer. In other words the definitions don't define. If on the other hand we think of sentences as combinations of sounds that *start* either at the beginning of a discourse[2] or following a final juncture and *end* with a final juncture, then we can include all the statements above as sentences. So there is a considerable variety of shapes that make sentences *in speech*. As has been noted the shapes containing more than one word are called "syntax structures."

All these shapes are available for writing, too, and in fact when the writing is an attempt to imitate speech they are all used. Any printed play or the dialogue in any novel will make that clear. But when the writing is not thought of as an attempt to reproduce speech, when it is prepared for the purpose of reading silently—in other words when it is really writing and not imitation speech—there is a distinct decrease in the number of available sentence forms. It is necessary only to examine the pages of a newspaper (except for headlines) or a magazine, whether it be *The Hudson Review* or *Reader's Digest*, to see that one shape of speech sentence dominates. This is the one illustrated above in the words, *He freed the slaves*. This type of sentence is probably used well over ninety-five per cent of the time. Only occasionally are other shapes started with a capital letter and ended with a period, a question mark, or an exclamation point.[3] This fact has led many grammar books to consider this type of sentence *the* sentence and to define the term in accordance with the characteristics of this type. It has also led to the term "sentence fragment," a derogatory name that dismisses all the other sentence shapes as improper. However, with our recognition that speech and writing are different practices and have different principles we can be more tolerant and say that in speech several sentence shapes are available that are not normally used in writing.

True enough, page after page of written English may contain no other sentence shape than the *He freed the slaves* one, and consequently we can and should concentrate on seeing that our writing does not use other random shapes as sentences, i.e., anything merely starting with a capital letter and ending with a period. But this does not permit us to condemn the other shapes, rather simply to recognize where and when they are appropriate. As speech and writing, which not long ago were rather far apart in their structures, get closer together, a greater tolerance for the other sentence shapes in writing will develop. But as of now it is safe to say that people learning to write in school and college would be well advised to train themselves to write no sentences that are not in the same class with *He freed the slaves*.

In addition to this particular word structure, there are two other similar ones. These three structures we shall call "nuclear sentences." One of the three has two sub-structures, and each of them has numerous "transformations."

def.   Transformations are special rearrangements and form changes of the words of a syntax structure. Sometimes the rearrangement requires the addition of one or more of a small number of words and a change in punctuation. Using the sentence *He freed the slaves* as a base, transformations such as *The slaves were freed by him, He did not free the slaves, Did he free the slaves? He freed the slaves, didn't he?* are common and normal. Other more unusual ones may be developed. For example, *He the slaves freed* or *The slaves freed he*. These are distinctly abnormal and need not be discussed in a grammar of *normal* written English. The usual transformations are quite familiar to all native speakers and writers of English. Of course in using the language for speaking and writing, people do not actually start with a base sentence and change it to some other form. Since the form they intend to use is available in their stock of patterns, they use it. Not everyone has the same stock of patterns. The transformation *Not slaves did he free* is quite probably in the stock of relatively few people. Consequently, though it has been used many times it is not for most people normal. The *system* of transformations will be discussed in Chapter X.

NUCLEAR SENTENCE TYPE A

A 1. Students write themes.

This sentence contains the minimum number of words for this type. The meaning desired cannot be conveyed at all if any one of the three words is removed. Either no meaning or a different meaning results. *Write themes* means something, but it doesn't fit the meaning that is expressed in the original. *Students write* also means something, but it is something else than *Students write themes.* The minimum number of words in a Type A nuclear sentence is three.

The first of the three words is called the "subject" (S). The other two words taken together are called the "predicate" (P). We can therefore divide the sentence like this:

$$|S| \qquad |P|$$
$$\text{Students write themes.}^4$$

All three types of nuclear sentences may be divided this way.[5] The possibility of being divided into two parts is what the nuclear sentences have in common. It permits us to consider them a single class of structure.

But we can also divide our predicate into two parts, the first of which is called "verb" (V), the other "object" (O_2)[6] thus:

$$|S| \qquad |V| \qquad |O_2|^6$$
$$\text{Students write themes.}$$

The general statement for this sort of sentence is $|S| \quad |V| \quad |O_2|$.

Some other things may be noticed about the sentence. First, it is an action sentence, and second, the action moves from left to right

action sentence
action moves left → right
arrives at goal

and—so to speak—arrives at a goal that is named. We might describe the sentence as containing actor-action-goal.

In most written English thirty to forty per cent of all the sentences are reducible to this particular nuclear sentence.

In addition to the three-part sentence |S| |V| |O$_2$| we also have two four-part Type A sentences. They are like the |S| |V| |O$_2$| sentences because they have subjects, verbs and objects and because they are action sentences with a goal expressed for the action.

The difference lies in the nature of the goal. In sub-types 2 and 3 the goal is not a simple one; it is complex. Illustrations of minimum versions of these sub-types are

> A 2. Parents give children gifts.
>
> A 3. Parents make children happy
> slaves.

Notice that there are four parts here instead of three and that if we take the third part away from A 2 and the fourth part away from A 3, we have simple Type A 1 sentences with a quite different meaning. So these two sub-types are simply A 1 sentences with more complex objects but not the same kind of complex object.

In A 2 we notice: (a) that *children* and *gifts* do not stand for the same thing; (b) that instead of using *children* in this particular position we may say *to children* if we put the words on the other side of *gifts*; (c) that we cannot change the positions of *children* and *gifts* without changing the meaning drastically. Since *children* comes first we will call it O$_1$,[7] which explains why we had O$_2$ in Type A 1. Type A 2 will be represented thus:

$$|S| \qquad |V| \qquad |O_1| \qquad |O_2|$$
Parents give children gifts.

In A 3 we notice: (a) that *children* and either *happy* or *slaves* stand for the same thing, i.e., that it is the children who are *happy* or are *slaves;* (b) that the position of the two words is fixed and that changing their positions makes the sentence mean something else; (c) that, as a matter of fact, the words *children happy* or *children slaves* are equivalent to the nuclear Type C sentence described below. For this last reason we will designate the fourth part by the same symbol as the third part of Type C, which is C.[8] The parts of Type A 3 are

$$|S| \quad |V| \quad |O_2| \quad |C|$$

Parents   make   children   happy
slaves.

It is necessary to use both *happy* and *slaves* in our illustration, because we cannot put the words that appear in this position in the same class. This will be discussed later. For the present we will say that C may be represented by words that are like *happy* and also by words that are like *slaves*. Everyone knows enough of these two kinds of words to practice with.

NUCLEAR SENTENCE TYPE B

Type B sentences have only two parts. They are illustrated by such a sentence as

$$|S| \quad |V|$$

Men work.

Since these words resemble S and V in Type A we have so labeled them. We notice: (a) that S|P is the same as S|V in this sentence, for there are only two parts; (b) that this is an action sentence but that no goal of the action is expressed. If we express a goal we have a Type A sentence. About fifteen to twenty-five per cent of written sentences are reducible to this nuclear type.

NUCLEAR SENTENCE TYPE C

Type C sentences are illustrated by such a sentence as:

$$|S| \quad |V| \quad |C|$$

Children   are   happy
slaves.

Two of the same words that appear in Type A 3 are used in order to emphasize the likeness of this type to the |O₂| |C| part of Type A 3. We notice: (a) that there are three parts; (b) that this is not an action sentence but a static sentence; (c) that the effect of the sentence is to put the first word into a class named by the third word. This is true even in such sentences as *That man is John Dunkel* because *John Dunkel* is (presumably) the member of a one-member class. This type is used almost as frequently as Type A.

A peculiar feature of this nuclear sentence type is that only a limited number of words (verbs) may occupy the |V| position. These words are *be, seem, become,* or words for which one of these three may be substituted. The difficulty, of course, is to know for what words these three *can* be substituted. In general, however, this is a useful criterion. For example:

> The door stood open. (stood = was)
> The grass grew green. (grew = became)
> The woman looked tired. (looked = seemed)

These are the three nuclear sentence types. Two are action sentences; one with an expressed goal for the action, the other with no expressed goal. The third is a classifying sentence without any action. Each type and sub-type has a minimum number of words, beyond which it cannot be reduced without changing or destroying the meaning. Each has a fixed word order that must be recognizable as a norm even when the order is changed. In a sentence such as *Children John hated,* we must recognize what the normal order is before we can understand the sentence.

In order to be certain about these nuclear sentences, you should not only write a great many examples of each kind, but you should examine a great many printed sentences with the aim of identifying which of the subject-predicate combinations are identical with the nuclear types and which are not. You will later on learn to recognize that the sentences that are not identical to the nuclear sentences are reducible to one of the types. Learn to eliminate all the words in the sentences that are not essential to the most simply stated version of the meaning. For example:

Spraying for Dutch elm disease began in a small way on the university campus in 1954.

When we look at this sentence we must keep in mind the way the three types of nuclear sentences sound and look and try to see a combination of two, three or four words that resembles one of the three types. If we can find an action word we can start from that. In this sentence two words seem to be concerned with doing something. They are *spraying* and *began* of course. We tentatively put each of these down as |V|:

Spraying
began

We then look for a possible |S| since we must have an |S| as well as a |V| to make a nuclear sentence. We shall expect to find it to the left of |V|. Since *spraying* starts the sentence we might at least temporarily eliminate it as a |V|. But when we ask what word goes with *began* as *students* goes with *write* in *Students write themes,* we find that *spraying* is the most comfortable fit. So we fill in our |S|-position:

|S| |V| ?
Spraying began _____

Now we must determine if any O_1, O_2 or C occurs. There seems no word or words that fit the relationship we have noticed in the nuclear types. We conclude that the sentence above is an example of type B and that its nucleus is *spraying began* and that all the other words are supplementary to the nucleus. By practicing this a few minutes a day for a week or two you can pick out the nuclear sentences from the longer sentences without fail. Of course there are a few cautions to be observed.

1. You will find many sentences that appear not to have the |S| |V| or |S| |V| $|O_2|$ or |S| |V| |C| relationship in them at all, though there may be some resemblance to these types. These sentences are probably transformations. This situation is to be expected. Don't try to force the sentences into a nuclear type. Pay attention only to

those sentences where you can easily detect the proper word order and the proper relationship.

2. You will find sentences in which the |V| contains more than one word and in which the meaning of the nuclear sentences requires all the |V| words. In *He has been writing letters,* we have a Type A 1 sentence, but it cannot be reduced to three words without distorting or destroying the intended meaning. The |V| in this sentence is *has been writing,* and the three words are a single unit.

3. You will also find that |S|, |O₁|, |O₂| and |C| may consist of several words that seem to be not reducible. For example: *To receive a letter is fun* is clearly a Type C nuclear sentence and what is placed in the class of "fun" is the meaning of the group of words *To receive a letter.* This cannot be reduced further; the simple |S| of the nuclear sentence is *To receive a letter.* In the sentence *He saw that I had finished* the whole group *that I had finished* is the |O₂| of the Type A 1 sentence—no part of it can be removed without breaking down the meaning. (Incidentally *that I had finished* contains a nuclear sentence of the B type. If you can identify these included groups, do so, but don't expect to see them all.)

4. It makes the nuclear sentences sound more natural if the following words are retained when they occur in front of an |S| an |O₁|, an |O₂| or a |C|: *a, an, the, my, your, his, her, its, our, their.*

The main purpose of this practice is simply to plant firmly in one's mind the relationship among the parts of each nuclear sentence type as expressed in different words.

• EXERCISES

1. Find and write out the simple nuclear sentences for twenty-five sentences of each type. You may use any available printed material: a textbook, a newspaper, a magazine, etc. Write each nuclear sentence with larger than normal spaces between the parts, as in the following sample. Then write the appropriate symbol over each part, enclosing the symbol in vertical lines. Make the lines distinctly longer than the letters are high. This makes them more legible. Here is an example:

After a good deal of difficulty regarding passports,
the spy finally got permission to cross the border.

Beginning with the word *got,* which seems like a V, we find *the spy* as subject and *permission* as object. We write

$$|S| \qquad |V| \qquad |O_2|$$
The spy   got   permission.

2. Write twenty-five original examples of each type of nuclear sentence, separating the parts by larger than normal spaces and writing the appropriate symbols (enclosed by vertical lines) above the parts of the sentence.
3. Using the printed version of a modern play, find twenty examples of groups of words punctuated as sentences that are not nuclear. Write each one out and add whatever words are necessary to make the sentence conform to one of the nuclear types. Assign each one of the sentences to its appropriate nuclear class.
Example:

"Where's the caviar?"
"In the refrigerator."

In the refrigerator is not a nuclear sentence. Adding the words *It is* would make it a nuclear sentence B.
4. Write a 300–400 word theme on a subject given by the instructor. When you hand it in, hand in also a list of the nuclear sentences of your theme, reduced to their simplest forms and properly divided and labeled.

CHAPTER V

Classifying Words I: Parts of Speech

The words of written English may be usefully divided into two groups. These groups may be labeled "parts of speech" and "function words." One obvious difference between the two groups is in quantity. The number of words possible to include in the category parts of speech is limited only by the permissible arrangements of phonemes. An English word starting with /tl/ or /ŋ/ is hard to imagine, but even if the peculiar inhibitions of the English phonemic system are observed, the possibilities for English words, while not infinite, are tremendous. These parts of speech are three in number, and they are called by familiar names: *noun, verb* and *modifier.*

Function words, like parts of speech, may be divided into classes. In this book the classes number six. Function words are limited in number, though it would be very difficult to give an exact number for any one class of function words. This is due to the changing of word shapes from one class to another. An example would be the shape *than,* which we find in such sentences as

Horses can run faster than people.

The last two words of this sentence have been most frequently thought of as consisting of a connective followed by an S that has an unexpressed (understood) V, i.e., *can run.* But these last two words (*than people*) look very much like structures such as *for people, with people,* etc., which obviously could not have verbs after them. The question arises whether to classify *than* as one kind of connective

(conjunction) or another kind (preposition). Of course no serious problem occurs unless we use such a word as *they*. In such a case it is
necessary to decide between two possible allomorphs. If the word
is thought of as an S then the appropriate form for written English is
they. If, however, *than* is considered equivalent to *for* or *with,* the form
them is appropriate. Traditionally *they* has been preferred. But *them*
is a great deal used, and if *than* is followed by *them* it must be classed
(even if the classifier considers the use inappropriate) along with *for*
and *with.* Thus *than* may appear in two different lists of function
words.

One basis for dividing words into the two groups (parts of
speech and function words) is the discrepancy in their numbers. Another basis depends on distribution. All those words that can appear
by themselves in nuclear sentences as S, V, O_1, O_2 or C are parts of
speech. However, not all word shapes classified as modifiers can appear
as C in nuclear sentences A 3 and C. Thus this basis of division is not
wholly accurate. Furthermore a shape *may* appear as a function word
in one context and as a part of speech in another. For the purposes
of classification, however, the division is useful.

A third difference between the groups is relative permanence.
Parts of speech tend to appear and disappear, though of course many
like *father, mother* have existed probably as long as has the language.
But a glance at a piece of writing done a couple of hundred years
ago will make clear that many word shapes that have always been
classified as parts of speech and not as function words are no longer
in our normal vocabulary. We have to learn them as we do the
vocabulary of a foreign language. For example, on one page of
Swift's *Tale of a Tub* (1704) I notice the following parts of speech
that are no longer alive: *coil*—meaning *disturbance; liquorish*—meaning *lustfully desirous; castoff*—meaning *wretch; parcel*—meaning
group. On the other hand every one of the function words is easy
enough to understand, though one or two sound slightly old-fashioned.
Parts of speech tend to appear and disappear in accordance with the
"things" to be named or described or commented on, while function
words tend to remain relatively stable. This may in part be due to
the fact that function words usually describe relationships between
other words or describe the attitude of the writer. The things dis-

appear, the relationships and attitudes are much more permanent.

Thus function words differ from parts of speech by (a) number of items, (b) distribution, (c) relative permanence. The division is not completely accurate, and there will always be problems of classification in regard to individual word shapes.

In the following discussion we will deal first with the parts of speech and then with the function words, remembering that the separation between them is not absolute and that therefore many shapes may be classified as both.

WHY BOTHER WITH CLASSIFICATIONS?

If classification of words is both difficult and imprecise, why is it desirable to undertake it? The answer is that in spite of the difficulty and the lack of preciseness, lack of any classification would be even more troublesome. Merely to identify what particular word you are talking about would require a rather elaborate description of its form and distribution features. If, however, we can say of a word that it is a "noun" because it shares certain features with many other words, we are creating a kind of shorthand to express what would otherwise need a sentence or two. Convenience, therefore, is the primary reason for classifying. Why not abandon calling certain students *freshmen?* They could be described in other ways. But the classification of students into freshmen, sophomores, etc., is convenient. In all of our uses of language, classification plays a large part. Such a word as *tree,* for instance, is a very useful word. Without it we would be put to all kinds of difficulty in talking about certain individual objects. Yet we can never be quite sure what a *tree* is. Deciding if a particular example is a *tree* and not simply *a large bush* is often a problem leading to argument. See for example Wordsworth's indecision in "Tintern Abbey": in "These hedge-rows, hardly hedge-rows, little lines of sportive wood run wild." But we should hardly abandon the words *hedge-row* and *wood* because on one occasion it was impossible to distinguish between them. Thus just as in other activities of our life we use classifications regularly and find that they help us in managing the phenomena of our experience, so in a description of a language, classification is an important feature.

In addition, classification, by focussing our attention on features of words, makes us conscious of differences that might not be easily evident otherwise. Thus it contributes to our understanding of words, which we largely attain by a study of likenesses and differences.

CRITERIA FOR CLASSIFYING

The principles on which classification in English is based are two. One of them is noticing the distribution of words, which means simply where we find words in structures and what relation they bear to other words. The other principle for classification is form, the shape or shapes that a word has.

Perhaps the most important feature of distribution is word order. When all other tests and signals fail this is the one we rely on. If someone wrote to you as a non-question sentence, *Deer bear offspring,* you would accept *Deer* as S, *bear* as V and *offspring* as O_2. This is because you have heard and seen this particular arrangement of words or structures so many thousands of times that unless some warning signal intervenes you will accept a three-word sentence-indicated group as |S| |V| |O_2| unless there is a reason not to. We accept word order as a device for determining meaning and also for identifying |S| and |V| and |O_2|.

On the other hand if confronted with such a structure as *Bear deer offspring* also uttered or marked as a non-question sentence, you would say that it is nonsense, because again we accept word order as a criterion for determining meaning and identifying the parts of a structure.

Furthermore if somebody wrote *On the table* as a sentence, you might feel that this was not very meaningful but that it nevertheless "made sense," because this order of words is a familiar one, and you suppose that there is a context that will give full meaning to *On the table.* But if the word order were *Table the on,* you would be completely at a loss as to how to ascribe a meaning to it and would either give up or ask the creator of the expression if perhaps he didn't have the words in the wrong order, or at least hadn't left a good deal out of his sentence. Word order is most useful to reveal the meaning of sentences and also to provide a basis for classification. To put it differently, the position of a word in relation to another word or words is a basis for classifying it.

The other feature used for classifying words is form. Form reveals itself in two ways. The first is by the existence of contrasting shapes that have basically like meanings but have certain sound or sight features that differentiate them. The form contrasts are fortified by distribution patterns in making classifications. An example:

    1. A *sweet* dessert.
    2. A cloying *sweetness.*
    3. People *sweeten* coffee.

We must all recognize that the three italicized words have practically identical meanings. Yet we cannot substitute one for the other, be-cause of the *–ness* in 2 and the *–en* in 3. It would be natural enough to put each of the three in a different class, and indeed there is no avoiding it, for each represents one of three part-of-speech classifica-tions. But this neat formal differentiation doesn't occur with all words. If it did, classification would be much easier. We could say that the shortest form is in Class 1, the form with *–ness* is in Class 2 and the form with *–en* is in Class 3. But a word like *blue,* for example, while it has a corresponding and contrasting form *blueness,* has no such shape as *bluen.* And a word like *shoe,* distributed like *sweetness* most of the time and like *sweeten* and *sweet* much less frequently, is the simplest form and has no contrasting forms at all. This kind of form contrast, though helpful when it exists, is not general enough to serve as a good basis for classifying.

The second kind of form is called "inflection." This is a change in a form that does not require a change in the classification of a word. This kind of form change is best illustrated by words that are found in the V position in nuclear sentences. *Sweeten* will serve as illustra-tion. This word has a series of changes (inflections) available. We may for example use *sweetens* or *sweetened* as well as *sweeten* in nuclear sentence A 1. We may write

    The men *sweeten* their coffee.
    The men *sweetened* their coffee.

but we cannot write

> The men *sweetens* their coffee.

We can also write

> The man *sweetened* his coffee.
> The man *sweetens* his coffee.

but we cannot write

> The man *sweeten* his coffee.

These illustrations show that the distribution of these forms is in part dependent on the S (which determines whether we use *sweeten* or *sweetens*) and partly on what the writer has in mind (an indefinite time or a time previous to the present).

With distribution perhaps the more important criterion and with form the secondary criterion, we can classify English words in a fairly satisfactory though not entirely foolproof manner. As Sapir said, "All grammatical systems leak." That is, there are always some items that do not act as they "should," either through historical accident, the necessity for avoiding ambiguity or some apparently inexplicable reason. We must accept these unusual items as the penalty for studying a technique that has not been learned as a system by its users. Chemistry can be learned as a system, starting from ignorance, but the use of the English language is learned by native speakers before they are capable of making generalizations, and most people, including, we may be sure, the vast majority of present speakers and all those who spoke it before 1600 or so, never consciously have learned the language as a system at all. It is not surprising that such an uncontrolled system should have problems that consciously created systems like mathematics or chemistry or even biology do not have.

One final question should be disposed of. This question is why aren't the words in English classified by one principle rather than by two? The answer to this question is difficult. We are able to classify all words that do not have changes in form or contrasting forms ac-

cording to their distribution. *After* for instance is classified in at least
three different groups, illustrated by the following:

> The boys came *after*.
> The boys came *after* the girls.
> The boys came *after* dinner had been eaten.

Each *after* is distributed differently, as we can see by inspection, and
each may be assigned to a different classification on no other basis
than this distribution.

But other words, which have form changes, do not seem so amen-
able, or else grammarians are so much in the habit of using form
differences that they are reluctant to give them up. It is the conviction
of this writer that some day distribution will become the only criterion for classifying words, since it seems that English can convey
any meaning it chooses without using inflected forms. Let us select
as an experiment a sentence from a famous author, Jonathan Swift,
which we will rewrite without using any form changes. We will use
only those forms that one would normally find heading a dictionary
entry. Here is the original sentence:

> And these people thought it a prodigious defect of policy among
> us when I told them that our laws were enforced only by penal-
> ties without any mention of reward.

Here is the rewritten version without inflections:

> And all this people at that time think a prodigious defect of
> policy among all of I when I then tell all of he that all law of
> all of I be enforce only by many penalty without any mention
> of reward.

It doesn't sound very pleasant, but I'm sure our predecessors in
the fourteenth century who spoke English as Chaucer did would consider *our* English quite outrageous. Our reaction to language is merely
habit. What we are used to sounds good to us. Anyway it seems clear
that as long as there are distinct inflectional forms some attention
will be paid to them when words are classified.

THE THREE PARTS OF SPEECH

Nouns (N)

If we take as a starting point the three nuclear sentence types we have studied we will notice that a single word such as *boy* can be used in all the positions S, O₁, O₂ and C.

> A 1. *Boys* play baseball.
> They saw the *boys*.
> A 2. *Boys* give their parents trouble.
> Men give *boys* instruction.
> An agent sent us these *boys*.
> A 3. The *boys* chose John chairman.
> They made the *boy* captain.
> He called John *boy*.
> B. *Boys* run.
> C. John is a *boy*.

Having observed the ease with which *boy* fills all these positions and having noticed that many other words fit equally well we can say there is a class of words that fills all S, O₁, O₂ or C positions. We will call this class *nouns.* But unfortunately there are other words (which may not be nouns for reasons we will later discuss) that can fill these places, and certainly—as we all know—word groups (syntax structures) can occupy the various positions. Consequently we cannot identify the class *noun* with the positions S, O₁, O₂ and C. We can simply say that nouns are words that *can* occupy these positions. We must seek further criteria for describing the class, since this criterion doesn't clearly distinguish nouns from other word classes.

Another feature that we associate with many of the words that we find occupying the positions listed above is that they are often preceded by the word *the.* And we also find that once we have been presented with the word *the,* we await the appearance of such a word as could be used in these positions.

The tall, old, stricken has an unfinished air about it. But if we add *tree,* we feel that some unit has been created. *Tree,* a word that is a noun, is needed. Therefore when we see a *the* we expect a noun, and we always get it. Another criterion for our class, therefore, is that the word *the* can be placed in front of its members and that the combination will sound and look familiar or will "make sense." Let's try some.

> The house
> The stream
> The swimming
> The discarded—Is this incomplete sounding?
> The red
> The go—Is this non-sense?
> The sweeten—This is non-sense.

Now if we try each of these pairs of words in various positions in the nuclear sentences and *if they fit* we can say we have established another criterion for our noun class.

Instead of *the* we can use *a, an, my, our, your, their* to test our words. These seven words we will call "noun-markers," and they form a special class among the function words.

If you will turn to page 91 you will find a list of about eighty words called prepositions. Placing any of these words in front of a supposed noun will be a further confirmation test. If the combination makes sense and if it could be part of a larger group, especially if it could be attached to a nuclear sentence, we have a third way of testing for what we can call "noun-ness." These are the best tests for nouns: (a) capability of fitting the various positions in nuclear sentences, (b) capability of having a noun marker precede them, (c) capability of following prepositions.

The other tests for nouns are based on form changes, and it is here that the puzzle and fun of classification become acute. Most of the words that we have called nouns on the basis of preceding tests have a way of indicating whether they refer to one of whatever they are symbolizing or to more than one. Usually they do this in speech by adding /s/ (/desks/); /z/ (/boyz/); or /əz/ (/baksəz/). In writing, the letter *–s* or the letters *–es* are used to represent the three sounds. The "more-than-one" form is called the "plural" form, of course.

If this method of indicating more than one were without exceptions, there would not be much problem here. But some words, mostly names of animals, use the same shape when they refer to more than one as when they refer to one. Such are *deer, sheep.* Others, such as *fish* or *tiger,* sometimes do have a different shape and sometimes don't. You hunt *tiger,* but you kill two *tigers.*

Then there are a few words that are relics from the days when English was able to show plurality in various different ways. Such words are *child, ox, foot, tooth, mouse, goose, louse.*

And finally there are some words which, being imported from abroad, brought their plural indicators along with them. Such are *alumnus, phenomenon, criterion* and many others. And to complicate matters there is often for these words an English plural as well as the original imported one. This is true for *antenna,* which when referring to the appendages on bugs is *antennae,* but when referring to the projections used to aid television reception is *antennas.* Other words with two different plurals are *radius* and *curriculum.*

At this point it is necessary to mention a group of nouns that not only do not have a signal for more-than-oneness but apparently can not have a meaning of more-than-oneness, because they can't be counted. Such a word is *gold.* These words are to be identified by the fact that they can have *much* in front of them. We can have *much happiness, much gold, much fun,* but we can't have *much baby, much tree* or *much leaf.* That is, words that can have *much* in front of them are words that name something that can't be counted. They therefore cannot have a plural form. But as is usual, many word shapes belong in two classes with different meanings. For examples we can say *There isn't much marble available,* and we can also say *The boy lost all his marbles.* But the shape *marble* doesn't mean the same thing in both sentences. In the first sentence it means a substance from which statues are made. In the second it means little round balls for playing a game.

There exist, therefore, in English "count nouns" and "quantity nouns," which can be distinguished by seeing if placing *much* before the nouns will make sense.[1]

But at any rate, most of the words we have been testing by our three distribution tests do have some way of indicating more than one. Therefore a formal test for most nouns is whether or not they can indicate more than oneness.

Unfortunately the test isn't so easy as it looks. For suppose a word passes all three distribution tests as *swimming* does:

> The swimming was good. (First two tests)
> He was fond of swimming. (Third test)

Yet it would be impossible to use in any normal way the form *swimmings*. On the other hand, *sinking*, which looks a lot like *swimming* —and is—will pass four tests. Are we going to say *sinking* (when properly distributed) is a noun and *swimming* (when distributed in the same way) is not? How many tests must be passed? Are the distribution tests enough, or must the form tests also be passed? If not all tests, how many? In other words we have what is called in sports officiating a judgment decision to make.

As a result of making a judgment, disputes often arise. These disputes generally result from somebody's saying that a word isn't really a noun. Here is where tact must be used. We must remind such a person that the classification of words is a convenience invented by human beings so that they can talk more satisfactorily about language. Therefore there is nothing sacred about classification. And we must expect when there is conflicting evidence that there will be difference of opinion. What we must do is to say "The evidence makes me think the word is a noun, but if the same evidence makes you think it is not a noun then we must disagree or else one of us must change his conception of what evidence is required to classify a word as a noun." In other words grammatical classification is not an exact science.

And finally many (not all) nouns have a form change that appears in writing as the addition of *–'s,* or *–'.* The *–'s* is added to singular nouns, the *–'* to plurals. This form is called the genitive. In speech the sounds made cannot provide a way of distinguishing this form from the plural except in a relatively few words that do not have the normal plural signal, such as *alumni's.* If anyone says /boyz/ to us we have no way of knowing whether he intends to have us understand *boys, boy's* or *boys'.* Since this is true it must be the distribution of the form that enables us to understand its meaning. And in speech the possible ambiguity as in *the boy's coats* versus *the boys' coats* has to be avoided by rearranging the words.

The genitive form is usually a modifier and will be mentioned in the section of this chapter called "Modifiers."

But the form is also distributed like a noun. In the sentence *Frank's is faster,* the genitive is an S. But it is a special kind of S. It means nothing by itself; there must have been a previously mentioned noun that we can supply. This is true in all the noun distributions of the genitive.

Not all nouns have a genitive form; the meaning is supplied for them by the use of *of* before the noun. Roughly speaking, only those nouns referring to persons or to animals have genitive forms. But this is not a rule, for we frequently hear or see *The car's motor is in good shape,* as well as *The motor of the car is in good shape.* At present no rule can be clearly stated about the use of genitive forms. We should probably prefer *The boy's foot* to *The foot of the boy,* but the latter would not sound especially unusual.

A sub-class of nouns—pronouns (N_p)

Pronouns are among those words that are distributed like nouns but which have some different formal characteristics. Because they are distributed like nouns and because distribution is the chief criterion for classifying English words, they are better classified under nouns than as a separate class of function words, which they resemble because of their limited number. The symbol N_p will be used for pronouns. It will be noticed that many of the words in the list of pronouns on pages 74 and 75 may be distributed in ways other than the ways nouns are distributed, but this is normal in English.

The principal characteristic of pronouns that differs from the noun characteristics is that they may not be preceded by a noun marker (m). This is not true when they are being spoken of as words, as in *This sentence should have a "he" instead of a "him."* When any of the word shapes that are listed in this section on pronouns are preceded by markers they are to be classified as nouns. For example, when we say *a mere nothing* or *just a nobody,* we will call *nothing* and *nobody* nouns.

A second characteristic of these words is that, like the noun-distributed genitives, they represent (stand for) either a previously mentioned noun or a potentiality identifiable noun. When we say *John is a good student because he studies systematically,* the *he* is clearly representing *John.* Thus the context provides the meaning of *he.* Sometimes the necessary context appears after the pronoun, as in *This is a good book,* where *this* obviously is given meaning by the following word *book.* When anyone says *I am Mr. Smith* his physical presence or the sound of his voice furnishes the necessary context. When we say *Somebody called* we assume that *somebody* is a person who could be identified. When we ask *Did you say something?* the *something* said or not said is potentially identifiable as certain specific words or sentences.

The pronouns, in addition to being distributed like nouns, also have form changes corresponding to form changes in nouns. In fact, four pronouns (*I, he, she, who*) have more different forms than do nouns. These various forms are best presented in a paradigm. In the paradigm on page 73 columns 1 through 8 contain the various allomorphs of the base form placed at the head of the column. The column at the extreme left of the table names some characteristic distributions of the form in the horizontal row. (These characteristic distributions are not the only possible distributions.) Blank spaces in the paradigm mean that the particular words or groups of words displayed are not distributed in the positions named by the labels at the left. The horizontal rows show which allomorphs of the various base forms are distributed alike. The brackets show repeated forms. The noun column (the last column on the right) is put in for comparison. It will be noticed that all the columns except 7 and 8 refer to single words. These columns show examples of two groups of words (groups 2 and 3 on pages 74 and 75).

Examining this paradigm in connection with the following list of pronouns that are at present used in English will make clear that most pronouns have only one or two allomorphs which resemble the noun allomorphs and are, therefore, very familiar. But four words cause a good deal of difficulty. These are the ones that normally in writing have a different form in O_2 distribution from the form used in S distribution. Since these are the only words in the language with this peculiarity, there is naturally a strong tendency to make them conform by disregarding this odd O_2 form. So far, partly because of

Characteristic Distribution	1	2	3	4	5	6	7	8	A Sample Noun
S, C	I[1]	he	she	it	you	who	this	someone	boy
Genitive (Modifier)	my[2]	his	her	its	your[2]	whose		someone's	boy's
Genitive (S, O₁, O₂, C)	mine	[his]	hers	[its]	yours	[whose]		[someone's]	[boy's]
O₁, O₂	me[3,4]	him[3,4]	[her][4]	[it]	[you]	whom[3,4]	[this]	someone	[boy]
PLURAL									
S, C	we	they	[they]	[they]	[you]	[who]	these		boys
Genitive (Modifier)	our[2]	their[2]	[their]	[their]	[your]	[whose]			boys'
Genitive (S, O₁, O₂, C)	ours	theirs	[theirs]	[theirs]	[yours]	[whose]			[boys']
O₁, O₂	us[4]	them[4]	[them]	[them]	[you]	[whom]	[these]		[boys]

[1] Notice that *I* is the only pronoun with a different form for each distribution. All others have repeated forms.

[2] Notice that *my, our, your,* and *their* are not only allomorphs of their respective base forms but are noun-markers (m).

[3] The distribution of *me, him* and *whom* is that found in written English; it varies widely in speech.

[4] The forms *me, him, her, whom, us* and *them* are the only forms in English that differ in O₁ and O₂ from the forms distributed as S. The existence of these forms is the only reason for saying that there is an objective case in English like the Latin objective case.

the schools, the forms still persist quite regularly in writing and somewhat less regularly in speech.

Who is in this paradigm because of such sentences as *Who is the problem.* Note the absence of a question mark. Such a sentence would occur after a sentence like *We must select somebody.* Another example would be *I know who,* where *who* represents something like *who wants it. Who* and its allomorphs are more generally used as function words (includers and interrogators), where the O_2 form causes the same trouble.

A list of English pronouns

This list will be divided on the basis of inflection. Using this principle one finds four groups: (1) the pronouns with no inflection, (2) the pronouns with inflection for genitive only, (3) the pronouns with inflection for plural only, (4) the pronouns with special inflection.

(1) Pronouns without inflection:

all	same
any	some
anything	something
both	such
each	what
everything	whatever
few	whatsoever
idem	which
many	whose
none	whichever
oneself	whichsoever

(2) Pronouns inflected only for genitive, by adding *–'s:*

another	neither
anybody	one
anyone	other
either	somebody
everybody	someone
everyone	

(3) Pronouns inflected for plural only:

(Singular)	(Plural)
this	these
that	those
myself	ourselves
yourself	yourselves
himself	themselves
herself	themselves
itself	themselves

(4) Pronouns with special inflections:

I	it
you	who
he	whoever[2]
she	whosoever[2]

• **E X E R C I S E S**

1. Look up as many animal names as you can think of. See how many have plural indicators. Can you decide on a principle of classifying the words? Is there any difference between those words that have a plural indicator and those that do not?
2. Think of as many "quality nouns" as you can. How many of them have a shape that indicates plural? What meaning changes take place when the plural signal is added?
3. Look up in three unabridged dictionaries (*Webster's Third International, The Century Dictionary, The New English Dictionary*) the following words: *antenna, phenomenon, criterion, formula, stadium, radius, alumnus.* See what is said about their plural forms and read the quotations given. Compare the statements of the dictionaries and report your findings in a short paper.
4. Decide whether the italicized words in the following sentences are nouns or non-nouns. In each case give the reasons for your decision.

We enjoyed her *singing*.
He thought her *charming*.
The reason for *resigning* was ill health.
Putting on a rough green is *exasperating*.
Making a six-layer cake is really *cooking*.
Copying your neighbor's answers is *cheating*.

5. How many of the words in the list of pronouns on pages 74 and 75 can have the noun characteristic of a preceding marker? Write sentences showing these words with a marker preceding.
6. Write sentences that will show how you are accustomed to using the O_1, O_2 forms of the three pronouns, *I, he, she*. Use both the singular and plural forms. Don't try to be "correct"; use the forms as you normally do.

Verbs (V)

In nuclear sentence A 1 the V in its simplest one-word form is a verb, and any word that will fit in this position and make a nuclear sentence is a verb. Nuclear sentence B, when it has a single word for its V, always has a verb in this position. Distribution as the V in one of these two structures is probably the best criterion for classifying words as verbs.

But these words that may be so distributed also have certain possibilities for form change that serve as criteria for their classification. The most significant is the possible addition of an –*s* or an –*es* (/s/, /z/, /əz/ in speech) when the preceding word in the nuclear sentence is a singular noun or pronoun. The contrasting form with a plural noun or pronoun is without an ending, the "plain" form, as we shall call it.[3]

The combination of the form of the verb with –*s* and the plain form of the verb makes up the present tense when an S precedes the forms.

Almost all verbs have another form change that involves for most of them the addition of a –*t*, a –*d* or an –*ed* (/t/, /d/ or /əd/ in speech) to the plain form. This form is used with all pronouns and nouns to make the past tense. Though this criterion is useful it has a good many exceptions; for example, a considerable number of verbs change their stressed vowel to make the past tense, while others both change the vowel and add a letter or sound, and a few make no change. Examples: with /d/, /t/, /əd/—*warn, warned; walked, walked; want, wanted;* with other changes—*sing, sang; bring, brought; sell, sold.*

Words that can be distributed as described above and that have the sound or visual changes noted also have a form made by adding *–ing* to the plain form. Moreover the plain form of all these words may be preceded by the word *to,* which forms with the verb a unit as closely bound as if the words were attached to each other. A few verbs, all from the group that make a vowel change to form the past tense, have a fifth different form.

And there is one verb in the language, certainly the verb that is used most frequently by all speakers, that has eight forms. This is the verb *be.*

The possible forms of English verbs may be shown in a paradigm using common verbs as illustrations.[4]

	1	2	3	4	5
3-form verbs	let	lets	letting	[let]	[let]
4-form verbs[5]	place	places	placing	placed	[placed]
	bring	brings	bringing	brought	brought
5-form verbs	sing	sings	singing	sang	sung
8-form verb		am[6]		was[6]	been
	be	is	being	were	
		are			
		[be]			

In summary it may be said that verbs are a class of words that may appear as the V in nuclear sentence A 1 or in nuclear sentence B (or in both) and may have certain form changes, the most important of which are the addition of an *–s* when the preceding S is a singular noun or pronoun and the possibility of adding *–ing.* These words have other form changes that are less satisfactory as classification criteria.

Naturally enough, the various forms have traditional names,[7] which can be used when they are under discussion. But it seems better, because more accurate, to refer to the various forms by the number of the column in which they appear. Thus the *–ing* form, which is often (rather carelessly) called the present participle, can be identified with complete accuracy as a "column-3 form," once the paradigm is learned.

In addition to the criteria of distribution and form there are certain word shapes that are indicative of verbs and these are at least supporting evidence for classifying. These shapes are most useful for classifying when there are contrasting shapes that are in other classes. For example, modifiers and verbs often have contrasting shapes, the verb shape meaning "to change anything so that it is describable by the modifier shape." Such pairs are: *red—redden, short—shorten.* But the usefulness of this sort of thing as a means of classification is much weakened by the fact that although many pairs show this contrast, others that seemingly should be parallel are not. One might think in view of the contrasting shapes, *red—redden, black—blacken, white—whiten,* that *brown—brownen* would exist. But *brown,* as the distribution and form criteria show, is a verb. Also since *short—shorten* is in existence we might expect a pair like *long—longen.* But here the verb does not come from the modifier but from the noun form, and we have the pair *length—lengthen.* It is this lack of consistency and regularity that makes word shapes poor criteria for the classification of words in English.

A note on the subjunctive

Although the paradigm on page 77 illustrates all the available inflected forms of the verb in English, it is possible to redistribute some of the forms in such a manner as to form what is called the "subjunctive." The subjunctive was once rather important in English, being used to express certain attitudes of the speaker or writer. Such attitudes as doubt, wishing, intention were expressed by a group of verb inflections that were distinctly different from the usual ones. Today the different forms have mostly disappeared, but certain of them have been preserved and have come to coincide with the usual forms. Such a sentence as *If he were my brother I'd be annoyed by what he does* illustrates the subjunctive. Notice that in this sentence *he* appears before *were* rather than before *was,* which is the normal procedure.

The sentence above illustrates the commonest modern use of the subjunctive. It expresses a contrary-to-fact condition—if the statement in the structure beginning with *if* is an impossible statement, the combination *he were* rather than *he was* may be used. It is however the practice of many people to disregard the existence of the subjunctive and to use *he was* in such sentences. Other possible uses of the subjunctive for modern speakers and writers are in such conventional expressions as *Long live the king* and in certain quasi-legal or parliamentary statements such as *I move he be appointed to the committee.* Thus it can be seen that the subjunctive has a rather precarious survival in English. Most of the ideas expressed by it may be said in other ways. *Long live the king* may be expressed by *May the king live long,* and *I move he be appointed to the committee* by *I move that he should be appointed to the committee.*

Nevertheless the subjunctive is still alive in English and must be noticed. The forms of the subjunctive are few. In the present tense the pronouns *he, she, it* and singular nouns appear with the V_1 form of the verb instead of the V_2 form of the verb. The verb *be* also uses the V_1 form with the plural in the present tense. For other verbs this involves no change, since the V_1 form is used anyway, but the verb *be* uses *are* in normal practice. In the past tense, the form *were* appears with *he, she, it* and singular nouns instead of the form *was.* Examples of this arrangement are:

> If he come early, I'll meet him.
> If the rabbit get killed, Marcia will be unhappy.
> If we be defeated, we'll lose the championship.
> If he were here, he'd defend me.

Notice that the first two examples sound rather unusual. Most speakers or writers would use the regular forms, *comes* and *gets,* in such sentences. It may be reasonably said that except for the structure *if he were* the subjunctive survives only in certain formal contexts.

The verb system of modern English, as far as the single-word verb is concerned, is not much different from what it was a thousand years ago. In fact, it has fewer inflected forms, though it has not lost any of the possibilities of expression, simply using one form in the place of several old English forms. The increase in complication in the English verb system (which has given it great capacity for expressing subtle differentiations in time relationships, in the speaker's or writer's attitudes and in the quality or kind of action involved) has come about by the use of auxiliary (helping) verbs, a group of function words that will be discussed in Chapter VI. A discussion of tense and the relation of tense and time as well as the way in which the one-word verb shapes fit into the total verb system will also be deferred until later.

• EXERCISES

1. Since many words that are normally nouns are also verbs without any change of shape, make some new verbs out of nouns that you have never seen distributed like verbs and write out the meaning of the new verb. For instance we have all heard of someone being *floored,* a verb that has the same shape in its plain form as the noun *floor.* Why don't we have a verb *wall* with the meaning "to put on the wall," so that we might say *He walled the picture over the table?*
2. Now make some new nouns out of shapes that you have seen distributed only as verbs and give the proposed meaning.
3. Now make some verbs from nouns by using suffixes.
4. Make some nouns from verbs by either using or discarding suffixes.
5. Using five different verbs write five nuclear sentences for each one. Each of the forms in the five columns should be used in a sentence in the proper way. Start with a 5-form verb and make all the other sentences parallel to the sentences using the 5-form verb.
6. Write five sentences for each of the eight forms of *be,* using the form as a V or part of a V in a nuclear sentence.

Modifiers (M)

The third part of speech is the modifier. This part of speech may be found in nuclear sentence C where it is symbolized as C and where it identifies a class into which S is put, and in nuclear sentence A 3 where it identifies a class into which O_2 is put. However, not all modifiers can be used as C. (Thus there are two classes of modifiers, as will be shown later.) Examples of modifiers:

Trees are *green*.
(That is to say "Trees are in the class that we call green things.")
We made him *happy*.
Boys often are *troublesome*.
God created man *good*.
The truce was only *temporary*.
That house is *occupied*.
This made the treaty *binding*.

Modifiers that occupy the final position in the nuclear sentences must be able to fill both places in the formulas "____things are____" or "a____thing is ____." Examples:

Green things are green.
Troublesome things are troublesome.
A temporary thing is temporary.

Besides their use in the nuclear sentences A 3 and C, modifiers are associated with nouns, verbs, other modifiers and sentences in a relationship called modification. Those modifiers not essential to the nuclear sentences A 3 and C can be identified if one is confident of the minimum syntax structures.[8] They are all the words that are not necessary to the existence of the structure, that is, than can be discarded without destroying the basic structure. In using this criterion anyone must be absolutely sure what a A 3 or a C nuclear sentence is like. In the following sentences the final words are C.

The little girl was beautiful.
The house is ancient.
Our children are alone.
He makes me unhappy.
The crowd thought him insane.
The new owner painted the house lavender.

In the following sentences the modifiers are not C. Test the final words by putting them into the blanks in "_____ things are _____."

> The owner is away.
> People are here.
> The boy wrote often.
> His life was over.
> People object frequently.

Since only nuclear sentences have been described we will confine our examples to this kind of structure.[9]

A nuclear sentence is *Boys played baseball.* This structure can be added to by putting additional words in various positions, for example, *Formerly the older boys often played baseball skillfully.* All the additional words are modifiers: *Formerly, the, older, often, skillfully. The* and *older* are associated with (modify) *boys. The* has already been identified as a marker for nouns; it is also a modifier. *Older* is situated between the marker and the noun; this is the normal place for modifiers of nouns when they consist of a single word or a series of single words. If we wanted to add another "modifier" to the group we would put it also between the marker and the noun, for example, *the larger, older boys.*

The first principle of modification is that single word modifiers of nouns normally are placed directly in front of the noun modified and between the marker and the noun when there is a marker.[10]

In our sample sentence the word *often* is said to "modify" *played.* Since *often* is just as close to *boys* as it is to *played,* how do we know it modifies *played?* The principal reason is that normally single-word modifiers or nouns precede the nouns. But this rule has some exceptions. Therefore the only real test is that it cannot be placed between the marker and the noun, as it could if it were a noun modifier. The combination of these two reasons is sufficient to justify our calling it a verb modifier. It will be noticed that *often* is not a modifier of *skillfully.* In such a sentence as *The boys wrote letters often to their mothers* the *often* can appear equally well either before the verb or after the O_2. When the pattern |S| |V| appears, the modifier may come directly after the verb.

The second principle concerning verb modifiers is that a modifier of the verb may normally come either before or after the verb that it modifies when the sentence is not a regular form of nuclear sentence A 1, A 2 or A 3.

Boys play baseball regularly. *not* Boys play regularly baseball.
but
Baseball is played regularly by boys.

Notice also that the first sentence may be written

Boys regularly play baseball.

and that the second one may be written

Baseball is regularly played by boys.
or
Baseball is played by boys regularly.

The varied word orders and the different limitations on the word order are the result of the necessity to make clear what modifies what by making it impossible for anyone familiar with the language to believe that the modifier modifies a word different from the one intended by the writer. The position of modifiers that are associated with V or with O_2 and O_1 is particularly important for two reasons. The first is that in English the relation between V and O_2 and between V and O_1 in nuclear sentences A 1, A 2 and A 3 is particularly intimate and that they must always be close together. This requires finding some other place for a potential modifier of the verb than directly after the verb. And second, since form is such an uncertain criterion for determining function in English, placement of modifiers where they can equally well modify—let us say—both the verb and the O_2 must be avoided. The ambiguity resulting from the wrong word order is a bugaboo for writers, for it often introduces a humorous touch in a place where the writer did not desire humor. This difficulty arises more with the use of group modifiers (syntax structures) than with single words, however.

Modifiers also may modify modifiers. In the sentence *He was entirely successful* we recognize a nuclear sentence C in which the word *successful* is a modifier since it identifies a class into which *he* is placed and since it fills the two places in *A successful thing is successful*. But *entirely* is not essential to the structure, which is complete without it. Therefore it must be a modifier, which since it is between *was* and *successful* might modify either word. If it modifies *was* it could quite normally be placed before *was* or after *successful*. Notice the difference between the possibilities of the sentences below:

He was entirely successful.   He was often successful.
He entirely was successful.   He often was successful.

The *often* can with equal ease come before and after the *was;* the *entirely* cannot. It is therefore reasonable to suppose that if the word doesn't behave like a modifier of *was,* it must be a modifier of *successful.* Modifiers can, therefore, modify other modifiers.

Modifiers may also modify sentences. An example would be: *Afterward the storm subsided. Afterward* in this sentence does not modify *the* or even *storm* (as *only* might do). It is therefore possible to think that the word modifies the *idea* of the whole sentence. In such a sentence as *He planted the bulbs carefully,* the word *carefully* does not modify *bulbs* because it is not between the marker and *bulbs,* and because it cannot be put between them without violating what we know is normal English. It, therefore, can be thought of as a sentence modifier. We may assume that if the writer of the sentence had wanted us to think of *carefully* as modifier of the verb (which is the only other possibility) he would have placed it in the other available position, that is, before the verb: *He carefully planted the bulbs. Any modifier that does not modify a word adjacent to it will be called a sentence modifier.*[11]

There are then modifiers of nouns, of verbs, of other modifiers and of sentences, which can be identified by various signaling devices and by various tests. The reader should be reminded again at this point that several of the syntax structures can also perform the functions that the single words we have been discussing can. The use of structures as modifiers will be discussed in Chapter VIII.

Formal distinctions among modifiers

Those modifiers that are added to a basic syntax structure and that are not necessary to the existence of the structure may be divided into several classes based on formal distinctions.

(1) The easiest classes to recognize are those groups of modifiers that have contrasting forms with some other group and are in complementary distribution.[12] Among the modifiers there is a large group of words that have two forms, one with and one without *–ly*. These are the contrasting forms. Most of these contrasting forms are distributed complementarily. Examples:

> There was a *quick* decision.
> The decision was made *quickly*.

These two words are distributed complementarily; no one would normally write *There was a quickly decision* or *The decision was made quick*. Thus two classes of modifiers can be distinguished on the basis of form and distribution. The forms without the *–ly* can be called "adjectives" (M_A) and the forms with *–ly* can be called "adverbs" (M_{AV}).

Some contrasting forms are not distributed complementarily; therefore it is impossible to classify them as M_A or M_{AV}. Such are the forms *slow* and *slowly*. While we would never think of writing *A slowly driver is a menace,* we can write equally appropriately *I drive slow* or *I drive slowly*. In other words we sometimes have a choice between two available forms.

All the rest of the modifiers have no contrasting forms. These include words like:

just	there
likely	no
soon	few
after	some

my, our, your, his, her, its, their
a, the, an
this, that
and all the numbers, cardinal and ordinal, plus many other words.

(2) Some modifiers have characteristic form changes that consist for one-syllable and many two-syllable words of the addition of *–er* and *–est* and for the rest the prefixing of the words *more* and *most*. Thus we have

> big, bigger, biggest
> pretty, prettier, prettiest
> soon, sooner, soonest
> few, fewer, fewest
> beautiful, more beautiful, most beautiful
> prettily, more prettily, most prettily

and some irregular ones such as

> good, better, best
> well, better, best
> far, farther, farthest

Naturally the numbers and the modifiers derived from pronouns do not have this characteristic nor do such words as

> no
> after, etc.

We can therefore divide the modifiers into those that have this form change called "comparison" and those that do not.

(3) Among the words that appear in modifier position and that do not have comparison changes in form are those that have shapes also distributed as nouns. These appear in such contexts as *the "shoe" salesman, the "meat" dealer, the "paint" store, the "floor" scraper* and many others. They include also the genitive form of nouns when it is distributed as a modifier, as in *the "boy's" cap, the "carpenter's" hammer* and so on. These may be indicated by the symbol M_N. These two kinds of modifiers come always before the noun and between the marker and the noun. Examples:

> The *flower* store   *John's* neighbor

The *shoe* salesman	The *principal's* young son
Tire marks	The *girl's* bright hair

The relation of such modifiers to other modifiers is interesting. When there are two modifiers, one of which is a noun that is not in the genitive form, we control the meaning by a stress pattern. For example in *the fine shoe salesman,* we make the meaning clear in speech by giving the principal stress either to *shoe* or to the first syllable of *salesman.* In writing, such groups are ambiguous and should be avoided unless it is possible to write the last two words as one or as a hyphenated word. For example: *The new car dealer* may be stressed *The nêw cár deàler* or *The nêw càr deáler.* In the first it is the *dealer* who is *new;* in the second the *car* is *new.*

When the modifiers consist of a genitive and another modifier, the genitive must always precede; if it doesn't, the other modifier will be related to the genitive rather than to the final noun. *Father's old shoes* cannot be written in any other order without changing the meaning. In other words, meaning is controlled in the first group by stress pattern, in the second by word order.

(4) Parallel to these noun shapes are shapes that occur in the verb paradigm (those in columns 1, 3 and 5) and likewise do not have comparison changes. Examples:

Column 1 (always with the verb signaller *to*)	Column 3	Column 5
A man *to remember.*	A *singing* bird.	A *written* document.
He came *to pay.*	The *writing* master.	A *required* course.
He was easy *to deceive.*	The *deciding* run.	A *planned* attack.

The normal distribution of these modifiers can be seen from the examples. The ones from columns 3 and 5 are distributed like those modifiers that have a contrasting form with –*ly.* The forms from column 1 are distributed like these and also like the forms with the –*ly.* But notice that the column 1 forms modifying a noun are placed normally after rather than before the noun. These forms may be symbolized by M_{V_1}, M_{V_3}, M_{V_5}. Some of the column 3 and column 5 forms join other modifier classes eventually. For example *laughing* with its contrasting form *laughingly* is a true adjective with a contrasting adverb. *Smiling, trembling, blushing* and others, like *laughing*, are no longer V_3 forms, but real modifiers. Such words as *determined*, with the forms *more determined* and *most determined*, have moved from the V_5 classification to the M classification. Other examples are *pleased, accomplished, excited*. A few short words may be found with *–er, –est,* e.g., *tired, tireder, tiredest*.

SYMBOLIZING NUCLEAR SENTENCES

Having provided symbols for the parts of speech, we can now symbolize the basic nuclear sentences not merely to indicate the parts into which they are divided but to show what parts of speech are used. Such a sentence as *Students write themes,* which we have been symbolizing as $|S|$ $|V|$ $|O_2|$, can equally well be symbolized as $|N|$ $|V_1|$ $|N|$, which specifies what part of speech is used for each element. As the sentences we discuss get more complicated we shall see what substitutes may be used for the simple Ns and Vs. Chapter VII is devoted to discussing what substitutes are available, Chapter VIII to outlining what the substitutes may replace.

Because many sentences have more than one nuclear sentence in them, it is necessary to distinguish the different nuclear sentences. This is done by placing a small figure 1 or 2 or 3 inside each bar that encloses an element of a nuclear sentence. Thus a complete symbolization of the sample sentences we have been using would be: (The ⟶ means "may be represented by").

Students write themes. → $|^1N^1|$ $|^1V_1^1|$ $|^1N^1|$
Parents give children gifts. ⟶ $|^1N^1|$ $|^1V_1^1|$ $|^1N^1|$ $|^1N^1|$
Parents make children slaves. ⟶ $|^1N^1|$ $|^1V_1^1|$ $|^1N^1|$ $|^1N^1|$
Parents make children happy. ⟶ $|^1N^1|$ $|^1V_1^1|$ $|^1N^1|$ $|^1M_A^1|$
Men work. ⟶ $|^1N^1|$ $|^1V_1^1|$
Children are happy. ⟶ $|^1N^1|$ $|^1V_2^1|$ $|^1M_A^1|$
Children are slaves. ⟶ $|^1N^1|$ $|^1V_2^1|$ $|^1N^1|$

Note that the basic nuclear sentences contain nothing but parts of speech.

• E X E R C I S E S

1. Write twenty sentences in which you use the following words as sentence modifiers, as modifiers of nouns and as modifiers of verbs: *after, forward, late, early, right.* Be sure that the verb and noun modifiers are next to the words they modify.
2. Write a ten-word sentence including the word *often.* In how many different places in the sentence can you put *often* without changing or damaging the meaning of the sentence?
3. Write twenty sentences using the V_1, V_3 and V_5 forms of the verb paradigm as modifiers of verbs and nouns. Write ten sentences for each, using a different word each time. Place some before and some after the nouns that are modified. Be sure you select forms that have not become true modifiers.
4. Write ten sentences using the genitive of various nouns as modifiers of other nouns.
5. Write ten sentences using as modifiers words classified as nouns that have no contrasting *–ly* forms and are not possible to compare.

CHAPTER VI

Classifying Words II: Function Words

NOUN MARKERS

Noun markers are word shapes that invariably signal a following noun. These shapes are: *a, an, the, my, your, our, their.*

Other shapes like *his, some, one* and others often signal a following noun, but do not always do so. For example, *That book is his* is complete and no noun need follow the *his;* but *That book is their* cannot exist as a complete syntax structure, at least in written English.

One of the most nearly invariable rules of normal English is that whenever a noun marker can be placed before a word in a syntax structure the word is a noun.

PREPOSITIONS (pr)

Prepositions are words that attach nouns or noun substitutes to a word or to a nuclear sentence in such a way as to modify the word or sentence. Prepositions are sometimes groups of words as illustrated in the list on page 93. There are about a hundred of them listed. A dozen of these do most of the work. An example of a preposition in normal distribution is *at* in *at the top.* If this is attached to the sentence *The man works hardest* by being placed after *man,* we get *The man at the top works hardest.* This is equivalent to *The top man works hardest.* Thus there are two ways of making a noun (or noun substitute) a modifier. It will be noticed that when a preposition is used to make a noun into a modifier the combination (called a "preposition structure" or a "prepositional phrase") comes after the noun that is being modified. If the preposition structure modifies a verb it usually comes after the V in nuclear sentence B, or after the O_2 in nuclear sentences A 1 and A 2 or after the C in nuclear sentences A 3 or C. It may come before the verb occasionally, but this is likely to lead to ambiguity, since the structure may appear to modify a preceding noun.

The symbol for preposition is pr.

The noun or noun substitute always follows the preposition except in one particular type of included nuclear sentence (see page 117). It is called the "object" of the preposition and may be symbolized as N_{pr} or if it is a group of words by _____N_{pr}. In the sentence *We rode with haste,* the word *haste* would be symbolized as N_{pr}. In the sentence *He wrote with a fine pen, a fine pen* would be symbolized as $\underline{mMN_{pr}}$.

Prepositions have no form changes. Many of the preposition shapes appear as modifiers or as other function words; therefore distribution is the only way to identify them. In other words when you see a shape that may be a preposition look for a following noun or noun substitute. If you find it the shape can be classified as a preposition.

The following list contains most (if not all) of the shapes you are likely to use as prepositions. A second list contains some that are not commonly used nowadays but which may turn up in your reading.

aboard	atop
about	bar (This mostly occurs in
above	the phrase *bar none*)
after	barring
against	before
along	behind
alongside	below
amid	beneath
amidst	beside
among	between
around	beyond
as	but
astride	by
at	concerning

down	regarding
during	respecting
except	round
excepting	save
for	saving
from	since
in	than
inside	through (thru)
into	throughout
less	till
like	to
mid	touching
midst	toward (towards)
minus	under
next	underneath
notwithstanding	unlike
of	until
off	unto
on	up
onto	upon
opposite	versus
out	via
outside	wanting
over	whatever
past	with
pending	within
per	without
plus	

A list of prepositions that you will probably never use in your own writing but which may turn up in your reading:

a	amongst	athwart
abaft	anear	atween
adown	anenst	bating
afore	anent	ben
amist	aslant	chez

circa	'mongst	syne
de	nathless	thorough (thoro)
ere	'neath (neath)	thwart
ex	nigh	'tween
forby (forbye)	o'	'twixt
'fore	o'er	van
fornent	re	vice
forth	rising	vis-à-vis
'gainst	sans	von
maugre (mauger)	secundum	whate're
'mid	sine	whatso're
	sith	

A list of some compound prepositions frequently used. This is by no means a complete list.

along by	in danger of	opposite to
along to	in relation to	out in
along with	in respect to	outside of
alongside of	in spite of	over in
as to	inside of	over on
astride of	next to	touching on
atop of	off in	up in
except for	on with	up to
excepting for		

• **EXERCISES**

1. Write preposition structures using twenty-five of the prepositions in the first list. Use a different N_{pr} in each and make some of the objects more than one word long.
2. How many of the word shapes in the first list can you use as parts of speech? Write structures to illustrate these other uses.

INCLUDERS (i or i_N)

Includers are those function words that enable a nuclear sentence to become part of another nuclear sentence, most often as a modifier but also as S, O_1, O_2, C. There are two sorts of includers. The first group, called "pure" includers (i), have no other function than to attach a nuclear sentence to some other nuclear sentence and to indicate the nature of the relationship between the sentence being attached and the sentence to which it is being attached. These are much like prepositions in function, except that they connect nuclear sentences to other sentences instead of nouns to sentences or other words. A list of these follows. You will notice that the shapes of these includers are often identical to those in the preposition list. This type of includer is often called "subordinating conjunction," but "includer" seems to be a more descriptive term.

after
although
as
because
before
directly
except
how
if
inasmuch as
lest
like (This shape is seldom used as an includer in writing.)
notwithstanding
now
once
provided (Sometimes this appears alone, sometimes with *that*.)
providing (This also may have a *that* attached.)
save
since
so
so that
than
that
though
till

unless
until
when
whenever
where
whereas
wheresoever
wherever
whether
whether . . . or not (This is a compound includer that may be
        separated by other words, We may have *He*
        didn't say whether or not he would go or
        He didn't say whether he would go or not.)
while
why
without (This form, as in *He wouldn't join the club without*
        his brother was invited too, is not uncommon in speech,
        but never appears in writing.)

The second group of includers are called "functional" includers[1] (i_N). This type not only provides a connection between one nuclear sentence and another; it also may be an S, an O_2, an O_1, a C or an N_{pr} in the nuclear sentence that is being included. Some of the available forms (*whose, which, what*) may also serve as modifiers in addition to providing a link between the nuclear sentences. The functional includers are few in number and their shapes may also be found in the list of pronouns given in the preceding chapter. These words are often called "relative pronouns," but this term seems much less clear than "functional includer." The word shapes used are

who (whose, whom)   whoever (whomever)
which   whosoever (whomsoever)
what
that

The includer that causes the only real difficulty is *who,* along with its compounds, *whoever* and *whosoever.* This word has, as has been pointed out, a different form (*who*) when it is used as S or C from what it has when used as O_1, O_2 or N_{pr} (*whom*). However, in speech the discrimination between the forms is made very irregularly by most speakers. Some of this irregularity has leaked over into written usage, though on the whole writers try to distinguish regularly between the S form and the other. It also should be noted that in order for these functional includers to appear in includer positions, i.e., at the beginning of the included structure, transformations are often required in the structure. These transformations will be systematically discussed in Chapter X. The only occasion on which the i_N does not appear first in the included nuclear sentence is when it is an N_{pr}, and even then it may.

Some examples will show the uses of the various forms. The i_N will be italicized and labeled in each sentence, but a fuller explanation of the variations will not be made until Chapter X.

We saw the man *who* made the disturbance.   *who* = S
We knew *whom* they had asked.   *whom* = O_2
He decided *whom* he would give the book.   *whom* = O_1
   (This would more frequently be written: *He decided whom he would give the book to*. In this sentence *whom* = N_{pr}.)
They asked for *whom* it was intended.   *whom* = N_{pr}
   (This can equally well be written: *They asked whom it was intended for*. This version puts the i_N in normal includer position.)
He forgot *what* they had elected John.   *what* = C
They knew *who* he was.   *who* = C

Other parallel examples may be easily made. Examples in which the i_N is a modifier (the symbol used should be $i_{N/M}$):

The boy asked *whose* farm we had bought. (*whose* modifies *farm*)
The little girl couldn't decide *which* kitten she wanted.
                                                (*which* modifies *kitten*)
We discussed *what* route to take.   (*what* modifies *route*)

These forms used as modifiers act like genitives of nouns and pronouns.

- EXERCISES

1. Write sentences using each of the includers in the list of pure includers on pages 94 and 95.
2. Write as many sentences as you can using functional includers without repeating the i_N.
3. Write a number of sentences in which the i_N is an N_{pr} or a C, illustrating your normal usage.

COORDINATORS (c)

Coordinators join two or more words or structures together. The joined words or structures may then be used as modifier substitutes or as substitutes for any of the elements in a nuclear sentence. Coordinators are also used to join two or more non-included nuclear sentences to form what is called a "compound sentence." Another satisfactory name for them is "coordinating conjunctions." There are only a few of these words. They are listed below.

and
but
or
nor
for
yet
as well as ⎫
plus   ⎬   These shapes do not normally join
minus   ⎬   non-included sentences.
times   ⎭

There are also the following combinations:

both . . . and
not only . . . but (sometimes *also* follows *but*)
either . . . or
neither . . . nor

The punctuation symbol ; perhaps should be added to this list, since it often joins two non-included nuclear sentences. Examples of the use of this group are

John *and* Jim
on the shelf *or* in the drawer
They waited *but* I went on.
They were late, *for* they missed the bus.
They couldn't get in; they were too late.
He planned *not only* a long trip *but also* an expensive one.
The child had *neither* food *nor* money.

• E X E R C I S E

Write at least twenty-five sentences that will illustrate the various kinds of words and structures that may be joined by coordinators.

INTERROGATORS (int)

Interrogators are those words at the beginning of structures that, in the absence of any contradictory signals, let us know a question is coming. They have the same shape as some of the pronouns and some of the includers. They are often called interrogative pronouns (*who, which, what*) or interrogative adverbs (*when, where, how, why*), but the simple term "interrogators" is better. Here is the list:

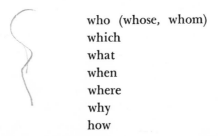

who (whose, whom)
which
what
when
where
why
how

The use of these words will be discussed fully in the chapter on transformations (Chapter X).

There are other question signallers. However, they are also auxiliary verbs and transformations.

INDIVIDUAL WORDS

a. Several words are always written out in sentence analysis and have no symbols. These are the two negators, *not* and *never,* the *to* that appears so frequently before V_1 verb shapes when they are not V, the $\pm by$ that appears as a part of the passive transformation (page 160) and the *do (does, did)* that is a question signaller. Notice that *not* often appears as –*n't.*

b. Interjections are words that play no part in the structure patterns but which almost always express the feeling of a speaker or writer. With these may be included *please, thank you* and their variations as well as greetings and farewells. Such words are not used a great deal in writing, but speech has a rich store of them, ranging from *alas* to *zounds.* There are also ruder and more blasphemous interjections that do not regularly appear in writing but are the most normal of words in the informal speech of males and increasingly of females. For the few interjections that show up in written English we can use the symbol I.

AUXILIARY VERBS (v)

Auxiliary (or helping) verbs are words that modify the meaning (lexical) verb. For example, in *He will go* the *will* modifies *go* in regard to time. In *He kept going* the *kept* modifies *going* in regard to the way in which the action is proceeding. *He has gone* suggests that the action is of present importance, that nothing has happened to change its importance. *He must go* suggests that the speaker (or writer) has a certain feeling about the action involved. Thus the auxiliary verbs provide for a flexible and meaningful use of verbs that in many other languages results chiefly from the use of inflections.

Two kinds of auxiliary verbs exist. One kind is the pure auxiliaries that exist only to modify another verb. They are called "modal" auxiliaries. These never occur unless there is another verb expressed or unless it is clear that another verb is to be supplied. *He must* means absolutely nothing unless the context, that is, the previous remarks or the physical situation, enables a hearer or reader to supply another verb. There is a rather limited number of these words. Here is a list of them.

modals

can[2]	ought (to)
could	shall
may	should
might	will[2]
must	would

Dare and *need* possibly belong in this list.

In a sense these words are like noun markers, since they always imply the existence of another verb; but of course the other verb doesn't always appear, as invariably does the noun following noun markers. In another sense these auxiliaries are like pronouns, since they sometimes represent more meaning than they express by themselves. But they have basically more meaning than pronouns, and they most often modify a word that later they may represent, as pronouns most often do not. These verbs are also peculiar in having no inflections. *He* as S does not require an *–s* on the verb in the present tense. This is the reason for including *need* and *dare*, which sometimes appear without *–s*. Examples are: *He need not go, He dare not lie.* Perhaps these are archaic forms that have somehow remained in the language. Nowadays we are more likely to say *He doesn't need to go, He doesn't dare to lie.* At any rate *dare* and *need* are different from the others, since they often have inflections.

In addition to pure auxiliaries there are also auxiliaries that can on occasion be lexical verbs (V). These present something of a problem because it is always difficult to decide when a verb has become an auxiliary. Perhaps the best test is whether the particular word needs to be repeated in order to give the intended meaning to the sentence involved. For example: *He had had the measles.* The two *had*'s in this sentence differ widely in meaning and both are necessary to convey the intended meaning. If we take the first *had* away the time of the action is changed. If we take the second *had* away the first *had* automatically replaces it, also changing the time. The second *had* is the meaning or lexical verb, the first one the auxiliary, having to do only with time.

If we adopt this criterion for determining a list of such auxiliary verbs we will arrive at a list like this:

> be
> be going to
> be to
> do
> get
> have
> have got to
> have to
> keep

lexicals

The combination of these auxiliaries in their various forms with a lexical verb (also called main or principal verb) gives to English an enormous number of available group verbs that can express a wide range of meanings. Most of these combinations are learned by native speakers early in life, though some people apparently never learn all of them. The so-called future perfect is not often used, for example, except in rather formal writing. The only way in which this large number of forms can be displayed in a sensible fashion is to see what auxiliaries can accompany the available forms of the lexical verb. We must, of course, recognize that V_2 and V_4 forms are never accompanied by an auxiliary, though this is concealed by the fact that the V_4 and the V_5 forms in many verbs are identical in shape. We must also be aware that it is quite possible to have as many as three auxiliaries with the lexical verb and that each auxiliary plays a part in determining the form that follows it. For example in the sentence *He must be going to jump* there are two auxiliaries. The first is *must,* which is always followed by a V_1 form. Thus the form *be going to* is compulsory. The auxiliary *be going to* must always be followed by a V_1 form; thus the lexical verb must be *jump.* In other words there is a rigid system of forming these group verbs in which the choice of each auxiliary prescribes the form of the next auxiliary and finally the lexical verb. Therefore if we present each auxiliary and name which of the five forms must follow it we will have a system by which all possible combinations (and some fantastically impossible ones) of the English verb can be arrived at.

The pure auxiliaries

The pure auxiliaries can be disposed of by a general statement. All pure auxiliaries must be followed by a V_1 form whether the following word is another auxiliary or a lexical verb. We have such combinations as, for example, *He ought to keep getting the bonus.* Here *ought to* is followed by *keep,* another auxiliary. The form of *keep* is not affected by the lexical verb, only by the preceding *ought to.*

The auxiliaries that can be lexical verbs

(a) The auxiliary *be* is always followed by a V_3 form or a V_5 form. When followed by the V_3 form, the group means "immediately relevant" to the time involved. Thus *He was working* says that at the time under consideration the *working* was in progress. *He will be working* is a prediction about some designated time in the future. When *be* is followed by a V_5 form, the word group is called "passive." This is the verb used in a "passive transformation," which will be discussed in Chapter X. An example would be *He was struck by the flying bat.*

(b) The auxiliary *be going to* is always followed by a V_1 form. All auxiliaries ending in *to* are followed invariably by a V_1. An example: *They are going to go tomorrow.*

(c) The auxiliary *get* is normally followed by a V_5 form and forms an alternative "passive" to *be* with the V_5 form. There is some difference in the meaning of the two forms, though it is not always quite clear what it is. *He was killed by the tornado* and *He got killed by the tornado* seem to be pretty close in meaning. Perhaps the *get* form emphasizes the action named by the lexical verb a little more, while the *be* form emphasizes the result of the action.[3]

(d) The auxiliary *do* is always followed by a V_1 form. But *do* has more than one meaning. It may give emphasis as in *He did finish his work completely.* Or it may be used to signal a question as in

Did you do what you should have done? Or it may simply ask for confirmation as *He got the job, didn't he?* In the last example *did* shows a common characteristic of auxiliaries. It stands for *get the job,* much as a pronoun stands for something. It also has to do with time as well as with question signalling. But despite the variety of meanings the following form is invariable—if there is a following form.

(e) The auxiliary *keep* is always followed by a V_3 form. Its meaning is that of doing over and over as in *He kept stumbling as he walked down the street,* or of continuing a previously started action, as in *He kept walking in spite of his injury.*

(f) The auxiliary *have* is always followed by a V_5 form. When the form *has* or *have* is used the group verb is called "present perfect tense." The meaning of the present perfect tense is that of linking the past with the present. When we say *He has gone* we mean that his going is as far as we know true up to the present. The form does not always mean "completion," as is often said. When the form *had* is used the group verb is called the "past perfect tense." It means that the action of the past perfect verb was over with before another action occurred in the past. *He had graduated from college before I met him* would be an example. When the combination of *will* and *have* (*have* is required after *will,* as we have seen) comes before the lexical verb, the group is called "future perfect tense." An example of this rather infrequently used group would be: *She will have arrived when we get there.* The meaning is that the event that the future perfect is concerned with will have occurred before another event also named in the sentence.[4]

(g) The auxiliary *have got* to means almost exactly the same thing as does *must.* It always is followed by a V_1 form. In modern written English it is not very frequently used, but it is common in speech. The form *had* is not normally used in this group. In other words, we might say or write *He has got to go* or *They have got to go,* but we should be very unlikely to use *He had got to go.*

(h) The auxiliary *have to* also is primarily a speech expression and an equivalent of *must.* It is always followed by a V_1 form. It differs from *have got to* in having a form with *had.* We can equally normally say or write *He has to go* or *He had to go.*

(i) The auxiliary *be to* is a form that has limited use, but is more acceptable in writing than the preceding two forms. It also has much the same meaning as *must,* though perhaps the meaning is somewhat less positive and determined; the act named is rather taken for granted. Like other auxiliaries ending in *to* it is followed by a V_1 form. Thus it falls somewhat between *must* and *will* in meaning. Only the forms *am, is, are, was* and *were* are used in this group verb. The so-called future tense and the perfect tenses of *be* can not be combined with a V_1. Examples are: *I am to resign tomorrow; He was to leave on Thursday; They are to start in ten minutes.* The use of *was* and *were* is interesting, since it results in a meaning almost the reverse of the past perfect tense, i.e., the action named takes place after another action also named but still in the past.

Experimenting with the possibilities of these group verbs is fascinating. Speakers and writers of the language have been experimenting for a long time. Some of the attempts have managed to get a respectable position in written English; others, like *have got to* have a precarious position, while still others like *had ought to* or *get to* have made little progress toward acceptance by the writers of English.

All verbs and group verbs in English carry an automatic time indicator. All present tense forms indicate general time. All past tenses indicate "before now." All pure auxiliaries indicate future time. All perfect tenses indicate time either before the present or before some other identified time. All the auxiliaries ending in *to* indicate future time. It is impossible to construct a group verb that does not carry in at least one of the auxiliaries some time indicator.

When two different times are indicated in one unit of discourse the normal signs are usually present. In the sentence *I have decided that I will go,* the times of the two verbs are past and future. In the sentence *He had gone when I arrived,* the times involved are both in the past, but one is before the other. But there are exceptions. Suppose we start with somebody saying *I have enough.* Later on someone reports this event by saying *He said, "I have enough."* So far this preserves the normal relationship. But it is possible to report such an event in what is called "indirect discourse." If we use indirect discourse we say *He said he had enough.* The second verb has changed from the form that normally indicates general time to the form that normally indicates past time. This change is usual for written English, though in speech the form *has* would probably be used as frequently as the form *had*.

A lot has been said about the use of the pure auxiliaries *will* and *shall* in forming the future tense. They are used, of course, to suggest a rather neutral attitude toward an event in the future. At present in the United States *will* is used in all sentences except in questions with *I* or *we* for the S. Even this use is not invariable general practice. If you customarily use a different practice there seems no reason for change either in speaking or writing. The auxiliary will not often cause any misinterpretation of meaning.

Would and *should* are used like *will* and *shall*, except that *should* has a special meaning of obligation, when it is equivalent to *ought to*.

Summary

1. All pure auxiliaries and all auxiliaries ending in *to* are always followed by a V_1 form.

2. The forms of *have* (*has, have, had,* either alone or preceded by auxiliaries) are always followed by V_5 forms.

3. The forms of *be* may be followed by V_3 or V_5. Which one is chosen depends on whether a passive is desired.

4. The forms of *get* are almost always followed by a V_5 form in writing, but sometimes by a V_3 form.

5. The forms of *do* are always followed by a V_1 form.

6. The forms of *keep* are always followed by a V_3 form.

CHAPTER VII

Five Syntax Structures

To be discussed in this chapter are five organized groups of words that, with the nuclear sentences, make up the units of the English language that either in themselves are sentences or that combine with single words to form sentences. They are the tools used in written communication. All six of the structures, plus a unit that is a single word, are illustrated in the following sentence.

S

|The little old house * on the corner *

V

which has so many trees around it * | |needs|

O_2

| some painting and some repairing *

to make it attractive * |.

The asterisks mark the division points between the five structures to be discussed in this chapter, and the vertical lines mark the divisions in the nuclear sentence. The nuclear sentence is an example of nuclear sentence A 1, i.e., $|^1S^1|$ $|^1V^1|$ $|^1O_2^1|$.

The little old house—headword structure
on the corner—preposition structure
which has so many trees around it—included nuclear sentence
some painting and some repairing—coordination structure
to make it attractive—predicate structure
The V (*needs*) is the single word unit.

The first structure to be discussed is the headword structure.

HEADWORD STRUCTURES

In Chapter IV, two groups of modifiers were identified. One was the group of words that could take the position of C in nuclear sentences A 3 and C. The other group was identified as being those words that cannot be part of the basic structure of nuclear sentences. The second group includes the first group when they are not being used as C. However, the nature of what modification of a word means was not discussed. In order to understand headword structures this must be done.

Put in its simplest terms, modification is the act of making more specific the referent of a part of speech (noun, verb, modifier or a substitute for any of these). It is essentially reducing the number of items that could serve to illustrate the words, the size of the area to which the word refers or any doubt as to the extent of the referent. For example, if we start with the word *tree,* we have an enormous number of items that could serve to illustrate the word, that is, could be pointed to as examples of what the word stands for. If we add the word *tall* we immediately reduce this number, and if we add a structure such as *in that field* and another structure such as *which has a dead branch at the top,* we presumably restrict our referent to a single example. *The tall tree in that field which has a dead branch at the top* is a headword structure. In this structure the word *tree* is the essential word, the foundation word upon which is constructed the whole complex of words. *Tree* is called the "headword" of the structure. Therefore this structure is a headword structure with a noun headword.

Another example, in which the headword is a verb (V), is *quietly walked,* which reduces the generality of the word *walk.* If we add to this, so as to produce *quietly walked into the room while her husband slept,* we have a headword structure similar in shape and thus in symbolization to the preceding one.

But notice that whereas the first example cannot normally have the modifier that precedes the N in a different place, the second example can have *quietly* after the V as easily as before it: *walked quietly into the room while her husband slept.* Examination of many of these structures enables us to make a generalization. When the headword is an N the modifiers that are single words normally precede the headword, and the modifiers that have more than one word normally follow it. When the headword is a V this generalization will not work. Not only can *quietly* be shifted, but the structure *while her husband slept* can too, as in this form: *while her husband slept walked into the room quietly*. Thus a rather rigid word order exists when the headword is an N and a more flexible order exists when it is a V. But there are limits. The units cannot be completely freely interchanged.

We can say:

> quietly walked into the room while her husband slept
> > *or*
> walked quietly into the room while her husband slept
> > *or*
> walked into the room quietly while her husband slept
> > *but not*
> walked into the room while her husband slept quietly

This last version changes the meaning by attaching *quietly* to *slept* rather than to *walked*. In other words it makes two headword structures, the second of which has *slept* for a headword.

When an M is used as headword the order of the modifiers is like that in the structures that have N for a headword. *Very happy in the park as he had expected to be*. The single-word modifiers come before the headword, the multi-word modifiers after.

The simplest headword structures are two-word ones such as *the child, work hard, very sad*. In contrast to this simple form we find modification structures ten to thirty or more words long.

Included among headword structures are multi-word verbs, the auxiliaries being the modifiers. It seems better, however, to treat verbs as a unified topic, as we have done in our discussion of auxiliaries (pages 95–105).

Symbolizing headword structures

In the previous chapters of this book a symbol for each class of words and symbols for the essential elements of nuclear sentences have been given. As we come to consider structures composed of words from different classes, we encounter more complicated problems of symbolization. Why bother to symbolize the structures and the more complicated sentences? The object of symbolizing is to demonstrate that even the most complicated of sentences is composed of the small number of units that we are discussing and analyzing, i.e., the nine classes of words and the six syntax structures. By symbolizing the units, the fact that the language is a relatively simple arrangement of a relatively small number of identifiable units is emphasized. It is important to realize that two sentences carrying vastly different meanings often may be constructed with the same arrangement of words and structures, and symbolization, by removing the element of meaning from the structures, lays stress on the nature of the process of sentence construction.

The two basic units of a headword structure are the headword and a modifier. The headword may be any one of the parts of speech (N, V, M). The headword may on occasion be a structure, though not very frequently. The modifier may also be a structure. Some examples follow:

the nation ⟶ m N (noun marker, noun)
the great nation ⟶ m M_AN (noun marker, adjective, noun)
the old white house ⟶ m M M_AN (noun marker, adjective, modifier, noun)
the peculiarly tall man ⟶ m M_{AV} ⟶ M N

(Here *peculiarly* modifies *tall*. This is indicated by placing an arrow between the two. When the modifier is a single word or a string of single words standing next to the modified word the arrow is not necessary.)

the dog with the white spot ⟶ m N ← (M)

(The modifier here is a group of words that we have not yet studied, so we will merely indicate it by a general symbol. Notice the parentheses around it. They mark the beginning and end of the group of words that form the modifier. The arrow shows what is modified.)

the horse that won the race ⟶ m N ← ($|^1S^1|$ $|^1V^1|$ $|^1O_2{}^1|$)

(Here the modifier is an included nuclear sentence, so we have symbolized it as such.)

$$\text{read rapidly} \rightsquigarrow V_1 \leftarrow M_{AV}$$
(The headword is a verb.)

$$\text{read with discrimination} \rightsquigarrow V_1 \leftarrow (M)$$
(Here the modifier is a group of words, symbolized by the general symbol for modifier.)

$$\text{read when they have time} \rightsquigarrow V_1 \leftarrow (\text{ i } |S| \quad |V| \quad |O_2| \quad)$$
(Here the modifier is a nuclear sentence with a connector—includer.)

$$\text{exceptionally pretty} \rightsquigarrow M_{AV} \rightarrow M_A$$
(Here the headword is an adjective, the modifier an adverb.)

These are the principal forms for the headword structure. Many more apparently complicated structures can be devised, but all include simply repetitions of the few units given here or substitutes for those units.

• EXERCISES

1. Using the following units, see how many different ways they can be arranged and still preserve almost the same meaning.

   I went yesterday to the park when I had finished my writing.

   (The "I" is here only to give a complete sentence to work with.)
   The units are: went
              yesterday
              to the park
              when I had finished my writing
   The last two of these must not be broken up, but for the purpose of this exercise must be used as single units.
2. Select five sentences from your daily newspaper, copy them and

determine and list the structures and the single-word units that you find.

3. Make ten sentences using each part of speech several times as head-word to a somewhat complex headword structure.
4. Change the order of the units of each sentence in as many ways as possible and record the resulting sentences.
5. List all the headword structures in thirty lines from the editorial page of your daily newspaper. What units appear most frequently? Write their symbolizations. What are the headwords? Try changing the order of the units composing each structure and comment on the results.

PREPOSITION STRUCTURES (pr N_{pr})

Preposition structures are so named because the first word of such a structure is from the list of single- and multi-word prepositions given on pages 91 and 93. The normal function of the structure is to modify, and thus it usually becomes a part of a headword structure. In many ways the preposition structures do in English what case-forms do in languages with elaborate inflectional systems, that is, show relationship and modification at the same time.

The preposition in a preposition structure is essentially a connector that attaches the remainder of the structure either to the specific word modified or to the sentence as a whole. But the preposition also has something to do with the meaning relationship of the thing modified and the modifier. The modifier is, of course, the preposition structure minus the preposition, i.e., the "object" of the preposition.

Any word or group of words that may serve as an N may be turned into a modifier by the use of a preposition. This means that not only words normally classified as nouns but also words usually classified as verbs or modifiers, structures such as headword structures, coordination structures, predicate structures, included nuclear sentences and preposition structures themselves may be attached to a word or sentence by a preposition.

Some examples will give an idea of the variety available for English speakers and writers.

With nouns: They arrived *in time.*
Others put the blame *on him.*
He was shot *at dawn.*
The book was given *to Edward.*
They traveled *in France.*

With verbs: (only column 3 forms are usable)
He had no love *for shooting.*
He had no hesitation *in complaining.*

With headword structures:
They put the chicken *in a small cardboard box.*
They looked *in the part of the house that has been deserted for so long.*
They walked *in the running brook.*
They decided *against coming to Ohio in the winter.*
Have some respect *for the dear departed.*

With coordination structures:
He waited *for Joe and me.*
The child rebelled *against the punishment and the disgrace.*

With predicate structures:
The rewards *for teaching school* are intangible.
He was an expert *at consoling little children.*

With included nuclear sentences:
Many wondered *about who was planning the invasion.*
Few students find much interest *in what I most care about.*

With preposition structures:
What did you say *about on the rocks.*
They kept talking *about before the war.*

This preposition structure is both useful and very common in normal spoken and written English. An ordinary page of print often contains thirty or forty such structures. The fact that they can modify all the parts of speech as well as the whole sentence makes them particularly useful, and since no form problem is involved in their construction except with the usual six words (*I, he, she, we, they, who*) they are very popular. They often serve as alternates for single-word modifiers and instead of O_1 in nuclear sentence A 2. Examples:

A *red-faced* man = A man *with a red face.*
An *occupied* country = A country *under occupation.*
They gave *the team* a dinner = They gave a dinner *to the team.*
He made *me* a new suit = He made a new suit *for me.*

When these structures modify nouns or modifiers they normally follow the word modified. Examples:

M
The army was ready *for the battle.*
  M
Unhappy *about her child's illness* the mother broke down and wept.
    M
He moved gracefully *for such a huge man.*
  N
The stones *in the road* are annoying.
    N
He needed the answer *to the problem.*

When they modify verbs they also normally follow the word modified.

V
She wrote *for a sample.*
V
The legislature reported *on its procedure.*

It is clear that this position is less subject to confusion than the position before the verb, since in that position the preposition structure might often appear to modify a noun serving as S. Examples:

N   V

The fire *in the chimney* started at night.

N   V

The fire started *in the chimney* at night.

In such a sentence as this the word order determines whether the preposition structure modifies *fire* or *started*. This suggests how fixed the position of these structures is. When preposition structures are "sentence modifiers" they normally come in front of the S, or after the O_2 or the C.

> *In the morning,* the news arrived.
> *After a long wait,* we heard the plane approaching.
> The boys wanted him *for a teacher.*
> The tree had grown tall *in twenty years.*
> Father bought the family a houseboat *as a Christmas gift.*
> They elected him governor *on the first ballot.*

• EXERCISE

Examine one column on the editorial page of your daily newspaper. List all the preposition structures you find. Identify the words and structures that serve as N_{pr} insofar as you can. Classify by some principle those you cannot identify. Submit with your paper the column you used.

Remember that N_{pr} may either be a word or a syntax structure of some kind.

Symbolizing preposition structures

The basic symbolization for the structure consists of a preposition and a noun that we call the "object." It is pr N_{pr}.

The only complications consist in variations of the N_{pr}. This may be a headword structure such as:

with a pleasant, kindly smile → pr $\underline{mM_AM\ N_{pr}}$

(Notice the line drawn under the headword structure; it shows that the whole structure is the $N_{pr.}$)

When the preposition structure is a modifier of another word, it is enclosed in parentheses as has been illustrated previously in symbolizing headword structures.

Other examples:

The army was ready for the battle ⟶ $|^1S^1|$ $|^1V^1|$ $|^1C \leftarrow (pr \ m \ \underline{N_{pr}}) \ ^1|$
The stones in the road are annoying ⟶

$$|^1S \leftarrow (pr \ m \ \underline{N_{pr}}) \ ^1| \ |^1V^1| \ |^1C^1|$$

When the preposition structure is a sentence modifier, it is enclosed in brackets.

In the morning the rain ceased ⟶ $[pr \ \underline{m \ N_{pr}}] \ |^1S^1|$ $|^1V^1|$

INCLUDED NUCLEAR SENTENCES

Included nuclear sentences are identical with regular nuclear sentences except that they are attached to some other structure or word by "includers." As we have seen in Chapter VI, includers are words or word groups that establish a more exact relationship between two structures than would exist if they were merely put down side by side. They differ from coordinators (c) in being used to make a nuclear sentence into a modifier or a substitute for S, O_1, O_2 or C in a nuclear sentence. Compare the following:

They agreed to help us. We gave them something to eat.

with these:

They agreed to help us if we gave them something to eat.
They agreed to help us because we gave them something to eat.
They agreed to help us when we gave them something to eat.

Each of these three shows a relationship between the nuclear sentences, a relationship that is unexpressed in the first pair. The words *if, be-*

cause and *when* are the words that make the relationship clear. They are includers. When they are prefixed to a nuclear sentence, they "include" that structure within another one. Often either of two structures may be included; the ability to determine which one would be more effective as the "included" structure is a considerable help in writing clearly.

Includers like the ones in the preceding paragraph are called "pure" because their function is to make the relationship clear and no more than that. But some includers combine with this function a function within the nuclear sentence to which they are prefixed. Fortunately these are few in number and may easily be memorized. They are:

who	which
whose	what
whom	that, and the combinations of all

but *that* with *–ever* and *–soever*. (*That* is frequently a "pure" includer, as in: *He decided that he wanted a blue one.*) By comparing a sentence that uses one of these with a sentence using a pure includer the difference will be seen.

> They wanted to know if planning was important.
> They wanted to know what was important.

When *if* is removed from the first sentence, we have two normal nuclear sentences. When *what* is removed from the second sentence, there is left one normal nuclear sentence and one incomplete nuclear sentence. This happens because *what* is the S in the nuclear sentence that it "includes," while *if* is not. Those includers that are a part of the nuclear sentence to which they are prefixed are called "functional" includers.

To complicate matters, however, *whose, which* and *what* are sometimes halfway between pure includers and functional includers. For example: *They expected to find out which man committed the crime.* The S in the structure beginning with the word *which* is clearly *man*. Consequently *which* does not play a part in the basic nuclear sentence, but is a modifier of *man*.

Group includers are preposition structures containing a preposition plus *whose, whom, which, what* and sometimes an additional word or words that form a headword structure. Examples:

> He didn't know *to whom* he would give his support.
> He asked John *by what magic* he had made her agree.
> They couldn't decide *at which motel* they would stop.

The group includers are often distributed so that the preposition comes at the end of the structure, as in *They couldn't decide which motel they would stop at* or *He didn't know whom he would give his support to.* When *that* is the functional includer, the preposition always appears at the end of the included nuclear sentence, i.e., *He asked if French was the language that she was acquainted with.*

A final complication will bring us to a conclusion. The includers *that, whom* and *which* may be omitted when they are acting as O_2 in the nuclear sentence that they are prefixed to, and *that* may be omitted when it is a pure includer. Examples:

> All of the people [whom] he invited have accepted.
> Many of the houses [which] the fire damaged belong to actors.
> (*That* could be used in place of *whom* and in place of *which*.)
> He wished [that] he had a million.
> (Here *that* is a pure includer.)

These omissions occur more frequently in speech and in informal writing than in formal writing.

Symbolizing included nuclear sentences

For those structures that commence with a pure includer simply put the symbol i in front of the first bar of the nuclear sentence, e.g., *When he saw the game* ⟶ i $|^1S^1|$ $|^1V^1|$ $|^1O_2{}^1|$. If the included nuclear sentence is a modifier of a word, it is surrounded by parentheses with an arrow pointing to the word that is modified, as in *He laughed when he saw the game* ⟶ $|^1S^1|$ $|^1V$ ← (i $|^2S^2|$ $|^2V^2|$ $|^2O_2{}^2|$)$^1|$. Or if the included nuclear sentence is a sentence modifier, it is surrounded with brackets, as in *He was amused when he saw the game* → $|^1S^1|$ $|^1V^1|$ $|^1C^1|$ [i $|^2S^2|$ $|^2V^2|$ $|^2O_2{}^2|$].

When the i is a functional includer the symbolizing is done this way: *He saw who was coming* ⟶ $|^1S^1|$ $|^1V^1|$ $|^1$ $|^2i_N^2|$ $|^2V^2|$ $^1|$. If the i is a group includer this is the process: *He asked for whom they worked* → $|^1S^1|$ $|^1V^1|$ $|^1$ [pr i_{Npr}] $|^2S^2|$ $|^2V^2|$ $^1|$. Or if the pr is at the end of the structure: *He asked whom they worked for* ⟶ $|^1S^1|$ $|^1V^1|$ $|^1$ [i_{Npr}] $|^2S^2|$ $|^2V^2|$ [pr] $^1|$. The broken lines in the brackets indicate an incomplete structure, of which the solid lines are the boundaries.

The use of included nuclear sentences

Examination of the examples above shows that included nuclear sentences that use a pure includer are most frequently M-substitutes, though they may appear as N-substitutes. On the other hand, the ones using functional includers are as often N-substitutes as they are M-substitutes.

• EXERCISES

1. Compose a dozen sentences that have included nuclear sentences introduced by pure includers.
2. Compose a dozen sentences having included nuclear sentences introduced by functional includers.
3. Compose ten sentences using *that* as an includer. From how many of the sentences can the *that* be omitted?
4. Write a symbolic representation of each of the following sentences.

> He saw what he wanted.
> Her father asked which college she was going to.
> They left when they finished.
> She forgot to whom she addressed the letter.

PREDICATE STRUCTURES

Predicate structures are, as the name suggests, very similar to the predicates of nuclear sentences. When the predicate is that of one of the normal nuclear sentences such structures almost never appear by themselves in writing, though in speech they occur fairly often, especially in answer to questions. For example: *What did you do? Planted a few bulbs.* Such a sentence as the second one above would seldom be written except when the writer is imitating speech.

Written predicate structures consist of V_1 and V_3 forms from the verb paradigm plus O_1, O_2, C or any combinations of these used in nuclear sentences. Examples:

> to make trouble (predicate of a nuclear sentence A_1)
> to write him a letter (predicate of a nuclear sentence A_2)
> to call him a success (predicate of a nuclear sentence A_3)
> to be an idiot (predicate of a nuclear sentence C)
> making trouble (predicate of a nuclear sentence A_1)
> asking me a question (predicate of a nuclear sentence A_2)
> making her a martyr (predicate of a nuclear sentence A_3)
> becoming a monk (predicate of a nuclear sentence C)

There is no predicate structure corresponding to nuclear sentence B since this type includes no O_1, O_2 or C. The V_3 forms often are preceded by *my, your, his, her, its, our* or *their*.

These structures appear as substitutes for S, O_1, O_2, C, N_{pr}, as modifier substitutes in headword structures or as sentence modifiers.

> As O_2:
> John wanted *to make much money.*
> He planned *doing it at once.*
> (This is rather infrequent; usually the V_1 form would be used.)

> As N_{pr}: (V_1 forms do not normally appear in this usage.)
> He spent the day in *reading newspapers.*
> After *planning his campaign,* he went to bed.

> As modifier in a headword structure:
> My brother, *wanting a new job,* went to California. (with N-headword)

He decided, *having surveyed the field,* that it would do. (with V-headword)

She was ready *to buy the dress.* (with M as headword)

As sentence modifier:

To study the subject further, they traveled to Italy.

As S in a nuclear sentence:

My being ill was a shock to him.

To write him a letter was dangerous.

As O_1:

He gave *learning the new language* his whole attention. (This is rather infrequent. Normally the sentence would be expressed as "He gave his whole attention to *learning the new language*," in which the predicate structure would be N_{pr}.)

Predicate structures must be distinguished from headword structures with a verb-form as headword. This may be done by noticing what type of nuclear sentence will result if an appropriate S is supplied for the structure that we are attempting to classify. The sentence *His instructor suggested writing a report* has a structure (*writing a report*) that looks like a predicate structure. If we make a nuclear sentence out of *writing a report* we get the sentence *He will write a report.* This is clearly an A 1 nuclear sentence and therefore we can classify *writing a report* as a predicate structure. On the other hand, the sentence *His instructor suggested writing frequently* has a structure (*writing frequently*) that also may look like a predicate structure. But if we change *writing frequently* to a nuclear sentence, we get *He will write frequently.* This is clearly a type B nuclear sentence; thus *writing frequently* is not a predicate structure, for, as we have noted, only the nuclear sentence types with O_2 or C provide predicate structures. The structure *writing frequently* must therefore be classified and as a headword structure with *writing* as the headword and *frequently* as its modifier.

Symbolizing predicate structures

Like nuclear sentences predicate structures may be symbolized in two ways, either to show the parts of the structure or to show what word-classes compose the structure. For example, *planning a new approach* may be symbolized as $|^1V_3{}^1|$ $|^1O_2{}^1|$ or as $|^1V_3{}^1|$ $|^1mM_A N^1|$. The structure *to become a good coach* may be symbolized as

$$|^{1}\text{``to''} V_1{}^1| \quad |^1C^1| \quad \text{or as} \quad |^{1}\text{``to''} V_1{}^1| \quad |^1m M_A N^1|.$$

When the structures are modifiers of either words or sentences they are enclosed in parentheses or brackets. For example:

the elephant, lifting his trunk ⤳ m N, ← ($|^1V_3{}^1|$ $|^1M N^1|$)
to make things certain they wrote a confirmatory letter ⤳

$$[\; |^{1}\text{``to''} V_1{}^1| \quad |^1N^1| \quad |^1M_A{}^1| \;], \quad |^2N^2| \quad |^2V_4{}^2| \quad |^2 m M_A N^2|.$$

• EXERCISES

1. Write the formula for each of the underlined predicate structures above.
2. Examine the editorial page of your daily newspaper and collect all the examples of the predicate structure that you can find. Write all the sentences in which these structures appear and underline each predicate structure. Write the formula for each one. The newspaper page should accompany your paper.

COORDINATION STRUCTURES

Coordination structures are groups of two or more words or syntax structures that are joined by one of the small list of coordinators given on page 97. Any combination of words or structures may be so connected, though written English is unlikely to use items that are too obviously different in structure. Almost anyone would hesitate to write:

Eating home cooking and to watch his mother moving about the kitchen gave him pleasure.

This no doubt is because *watching* could just as well be used and because doing so would give a balance and symmetry that helps communication in English.

On the other hand a sentence like:

They were either dead or in danger of dying.

is quite normal. We can say, therefore, that care must be exercised in joining words or structures of different kinds, and that in general such coordination structures should be avoided, especially when it is easy to use two or more words or structures of the same type.

The simple combination of two items presents few problems. But coordination structures often have three or more items. It is possible to express these by using coordinators between each pair as in *He is tall and handsome and blond.* But it is more common to omit the coordinators except between the last two items, i.e., *He is tall, handsome and blond.* This omission is always marked by a comma. The formula for this structure would be $|^1N_p{}^1|$ $|^1V_2{}^1|$ $|^1/M, M \text{ c } N/^1|$. The comma marks the position of a possible coordinator.

Coordinators are often double, as we see from the list in Chapter VI. Normally the double coordinators are represented by two symbols that may be marked with subscripts to prevent confusion. Using the same subscript indicates that both coordinators are part of a compound. Thus *big and strong and healthy* would be $/M \text{ c } M \text{ c } M/$ whereas *both young and beautiful* would be $/c_1 M c_1 M/$.

• EXERCISES

1. Make coordination structures using all the structures you have learned about so far, including, of course, the nuclear sentences.
2. Find all the coordination structures you can in one column on the editorial page of your daily newspaper. Write the formula for each one. If you find some you cannot write the formula for, list them separately. Submit with your paper the column that you used.

A SPECIAL VARIANT OF THE
NUCLEAR SENTENCE STRUCTURE

A structure exists in English that closely resembles a nuclear sentence, yet unlike nuclear sentences is not commonly written with a beginning capital letter and an ending period. This structure also resembles the predicate structure in using the "to" V_1 and V_3 forms. Like a nuclear sentence it has a subject and a predicate. Examples of this structure are the italicized portions of the following sentences.

We wanted *him to make the decision.*
We watched *them playing poker.*

In these italicized sections it is easy to identify the S and the P. The subject of the first sentence is *him;* of the second, *them.* The predicate of the first is *to make the decision;* of the second, *playing poker.* In each of these sentences the structure is an O_2 and thus resembles a predicate structure in its use. Notice, too, that the subjects are *him* and *them,* not *he* and *they.*

The structure, then, is one with a subject and predicate, the subject being in the "objective case" when it is a pronoun, and the structure is used as one element in a normal nuclear sentence. Of course when the subject of the structure is a noun, the problem of case does not occur.

Besides acting as an O_2 this structure is used also as the object of a preposition (N_{pr}) as in: *We waited for him to make the first move,* and *The delay was caused by him being late.* The "to" V_1 form with *for* as preposition is often used as the S of a normal nuclear sentence as in *For him to play the piano was a rare event.* In such a sentence the subject is a preposition structure. The structure with the V_3 form may occasionally be used as S, but it hardly sounds normal, e.g., *Him playing the piano was a rare event.*

This structure is symbolized exactly like a nuclear sentence.

In symbolizing written English according to the system used here, it is important to distinguish between generalized symbols and specific symbols. For example, nuclear sentence A 1 has a general formula $|^1S^1|$ $|^1V^1|$ $|^1O_2^1|$. This means that it always must have in it the three elements subject, verb, direct object. But a particular sentence belonging to the A 1 class of nuclear sentences will have a more precise and usually more complicated symbolization. Let us take the sentence *To solve a complicated problem requires a great deal of concentration.* The general formula of this sentence is $|^1S^1|$ $|^1V^1|$ $|^1O_2^1|$, but such a symbolization serves simply to classify it as a nuclear sentence, not to give a picture of each of its parts and of their internal structure. We must first therefore identify the three essential elements and attack each one separately. First we identify all the words comprised under the symbol S. S includes the words *To solve a complicated problem.* V on the other hand consists of a single word, *requires.* O_2 includes the remainder of the sentence, *a great deal of concentration.* Therefore:

S is a predicate structure consisting of the following elements:

1. *to solve* symbolized by "to" V_1.

2. *a complicated problem* is a headword structure consisting of a noun modified by a noun marker and a normal modifier. It may be symbolized by m M_A N.

But a predicate structure consists of a V_1 or a V_3 plus the following element or elements of a nuclear sentence of the A or C type. Thus we must symbolize the relationship as well, which we do by using the vertical lines and superscripts that mark the beginnings and ends of nuclear sentence elements, thus:

$$|^1\text{"to" } V^1| \quad |^1\text{m M N}^1|.$$

But S is, taken altogether, one element of a nuclear sentence and must have its beginning and ending marked, and each line must have a superscript. So finally

$$S \rightarrowtail |^2 \ |^1\text{to } V_1^1| \quad |^1\text{m M N}^1| \ ^2|.$$

V presents no problems; we must simply identify the word. Therefore:

$$V \rightarrowtail |^2V_2^2|.$$

Its separation lines have the same superscripts as those that mark the boundaries of S because it is the second element in the nuclear sentence type A 1.

O_2 is another structure that we recognize as a headword structure with a noun headword. The headword is a noun, *deal.* So we start with N. N is modified by a marker and a modifier in front, and thus we write m M_A N. It is followed by a preposition with a noun as N_{pr}. We write pr N_{pr} and add it to the previous symbols, getting m M_A N pr N_{pr}. Then in order to show that pr N_{pr} is a structure modifying the first N we put parentheses around it and add a light arrow pointing to the word that is being modified, thus: m M N $\leftarrow$ (^{1} pr N_{pr} ^{1}). The superscript is added so that we can identify this structure if, as it often happens, there is more than one modifying structure in the sentence. Then, since O_2 is an element in our nuclear sentence we must add the boundary markers with the proper superscripts. Therefore:

$$O^2 \rightsquigarrow |^2 \text{m M N} \leftarrow (^1\underline{\text{pr}}\,N_{pr}{}^1)^2|$$

Putting the three elements together we arrive at the formula for this particular sentence, i.e.,

$$|^2 \quad |^1\text{``to''}\,V_1{}^1| \quad |^1\text{m M N}^1| \quad ^2| \quad |^2V_2{}^2| \quad |^2\text{m M N} \leftarrow (^1\text{pr}\,N_{pr}{}^1)^2|,$$

or $|^1S^1|$ $|^1V^1|$ $|^1O_2{}^1|$ has thus been expanded to account for every word. For each nuclear sentence or predicate structure, then, there is a generalized formula (see page 124) and a specific formula.

As has previously been said, this process of symbolizing makes one realize that all sentences, however complicated, are composed of examples of the small number of units that have been discussed in Chapters V, VI and VII.

CHAPTER VIII

The Distribution of Syntax Structures as Parts of Other Syntax Structures

It has been made clear that S, O_2, V and so on are not by any means always single words. Most of the one-word units that compose syntax structures may be represented by some syntax structure. The purpose of this chapter is to list the various structures that may be distributed as items in the syntax structure formulas. We shall start with the nuclear sentence.

DISTRIBUTION OF SYNTAX STRUCTURES AS S

Every nuclear sentence includes an S. Structures distributed as S are various. In fact, all the syntax structures except non-included nuclear sentences may appear as S.

Headword structures with noun headwords

$$\begin{array}{ccc} S & V & C \end{array}$$
|The little old house| |was| |my favorite|.
$$\begin{array}{ccc} S & V & O_2 \end{array}$$
|That picture in the magazine| |shocked| |me|.
$$\begin{array}{ccc} S & V & C \end{array}$$
|The boy who played the saxophone| |was| |an orphan|.

Any combination of these may occur, such as:

$$S$$
|That big girl with the little dog, who is crossing the street,|
$$V$$
|lives near us|.

Headword structures with verb headwords

S   V C
|Writing with a pen| |is| |necessary|.

S   V   C
|To travel with your mother-in-law| |is| |unusual|.

Included nuclear sentences

S   V   C
|What he needed| |was| |a good meal|.

S   V   C
|Where he went| |was| |our concern|.

Predicate structures

S   V   C
|To conceal a spy| |is| |dangerous|.

S   V O_2
|Manipulating a mechanism like this| |requires| |skill|.

Coordination structures

S   V O_2
|My father and my brother| |own| |a farm|.

S   V   C
|Who they were and where they came from| |was| |uncertain|.

Preposition structures are quite unusual in S position in written English, though a few are common in spoken English. Examples are:

S   V C
|For him to lose his way| |is| |unusual|.

```
        S       V           C
    |In jail|  |is|   |where he belongs|.
            S       V    C
    |Over the fence|  |is|   |out|.
```

These are different from *Over the fence is a vine,* because they are statements of classification, i.e., *over the fence* is a member of the class called *outs.* It seems then that the qualifications for nuclear sentence C are met and that *Over the fence* is S, while *out* is C. In the other sentence the S is quite obviously *a vine* and all the rest is the predicate. Such sentences as *Over the fence is out* may of course occur in writing that intends to have the features of speech.

DISTRIBUTION OF SYNTAX STRUCTURES AS O_2

Since all the structures that can substitute for S can also substitute for O_2 there is no need to illustrate them all. A few samples are:

```
        S       V               O₂
      |He|  |brought|   |a book and a sandwich|.
        S       V           O₂
      |He|  |wanted|   |to go with us|.
        S       V           O₂
      |He|  |hated|   |what they had made of her|.
```

DISTRIBUTION OF SYNTAX STRUCTURES AS O_1

O_1 may be represented by headword structures and coordination structures in normal written discourse, as, for example:

```
      S           V                   O₁                      O₂
 |My parents|  |gave|   |that little girl who lives next door|  |a kitten|.
        S           V               O₁
 |Their friends|  |gave|   |my brother John and his wife|
                                                      O₂
                                              |a silver service|.
```

It is possible that included nuclear sentences and predicate structures can represent O_1 but this is hardly normal. Such a sentence as

S	V	O_1	O_2
|He|	|gave|	|studying Latin|	|a great deal of time|.

is meaningful, but a person would be much more likely to write *He gave a great deal of time to studying Latin.*

DISTRIBUTION OF SYNTAX STRUCTURES AS C

Headword structures, coordination structures and inluded nuclear sentences may represent C both in nuclear sentence C and in nuclear sentence A 3.

S   V   C
|He| |was| |the man in the iron mask, who had been in prison for years|.

S   V   C
|He| |was| |both a good father and a wonderful son|.

S   V   C
|He| |was| |what he wanted to be|.

S   V O_2 C
|They| |elected| |him| |president of that little club|.

S   V O_2 C
|The directors| |appointed| |him| |vice-president and general manager|.

S   V O_2 C
|He| |made| |him| |what he wanted to be|.

DISTRIBUTION OF SYNTAX STRUCTURES AS N_{pr}

All the syntax structures may be distributed as N_{pr}, though some are found in this position far less frequently than others. Headword structures with noun headwords occur most often, ranging from a simple *on the floor* to such a structure as *in the old stone Gothic church by the river which flows so swiftly through the little village.* We may also have as N_{pr} headword structures with verb headwords as in *after acting peculiarly,* or *in reading* through the book.

Predicate structures are fairly common as N_{pr}. Some example are

in *choosing a wife*

for *writing a letter*

after *criticizing the weakness*

It should be noticed that the V in the predicate structure is always a V_3, never a V_1 or a "to" $-V_1$ as it may be when substituting for S or O_2.

Included nuclear sentences are less common. Examples of the occurrence are

for *what he wanted*

because of *where he had been*

in spite of *when he arrived*

These distributions must be distinguished from the included nuclear sentences illustrated by *for which he has applied,* where the *for which* is a preposition structure serving as an includer. Nuclear sentences containing these two different types of structure are

He was welcome in spite of *when he arrived.*
$$N_{pr}$$
(In this sentence *welcome* is the headword of a headword structure, *in spite of* is a preposition, and *when he arrived* is an N_{pr}.)

He got the job for which he had applied.

(In this sentence *job* is the headword of a headword structure in which the modifier is the included nuclear sentence *for which he has applied* and *for which* is the includer.)

The two structures may be distinguished by moving the preposition to the end of the included nuclear sentence. If the meaning is not damaged the sentence is of the type illustrated by *He got the job for which he had applied.* You will also notice that the possible confusion only occurs when the includer is a functional includer.

Coordination structures are common:

> for *him and me*
>
> in *youth and age*
>
> for *either the best or the worst*

Occasionally a preposition structure may be distributed as an N_{pr} though this distribution is more common in speech than in writing. The structure

> *for on the beach*
> pr N_{pr}

is reasonably normal in such a sentence as

> They are suitable for on the beach.

But in writing such structures are quite uncommon.

• EXERCISES

1. Write as many nuclear sentences as your instructor requests illustrating the use of syntax structures as S, O_2, O_1, C, N_{pr}. Underline the words comprising the structure you are giving an example of, and divide the nuclear sentences into their major elements, labeling each one as it is labeled in the text.
2. Devise some sentences that will use predicate structures as C. State under what conditions this arrangement is workable.

3. Devise some sentences using included nuclear sentences as O_1. How many of the sentences you have written would you use in a theme?

4. Devise some preposition structures in which other preposition structures are used as N_{pr}. Devise some in which included nuclear sentences are used as N_{pr}.

DISTRIBUTION OF SYNTAX STRUCTURES AS V

Just as headword structures are very frequent as S and O_2, so they are as V. V always has a verb as a headword, of course, with included nuclear sentences, preposition structures, coordination structures, predicate structures and headword structures as modifiers of this verb.

V with a preposition structure modifying the verb headword

$$V \leftarrow (^1pr\ N_{pr}^{\ 1})$$
walked (with a swagger)
reads (in a deckchair)
will send (for a new catalogue)
has planned (in great detail)
is dashing (around the house)

There may, of course, be more than a preposition structure modifying the headword. For example, the combination of a single-word M and a preposition structure is frequent, as in:

$$V \leftarrow M\ (^1pr\ N_{pr}^{\ 1})$$
wrote sadly (to her mother)
asked quietly (for a ham sandwich)
looked often (down the street)
thought intensely (for a moment)

Many times, of course, the single-word M can occur before the V as in:

sadly wrote (to her mother)
quietly asked (for a ham sandwich)
often looked (down the street)

But *intensely thought for a moment* doesn't sound quite normal. We cannot therefore say that the single-word M can *always* be placed in front of the V.

Also the preposition structure may sometimes come in front of the V. This arrangement is infrequent, however, because the preposition structure might be thought to modify the S, which normally would come just in front of it. *John for a moment thought intensely* seems reasonably normal.

Although examples can be found of a single-word M and preposition structures both coming in front of the V, they almost invariably sound distorted.

And finally the positions of the single-word M and the preposition structure may often be interchanged when they both follow the V.

> wrote (to her mother) sadly
> called (for a ham sandwich) quietly
> thought (for a moment) intensely

In general we can say that there is much more flexibility in the positioning of the modifiers when a structure has a V headword than when it has an N headword. Rules stating the limits of this flexibility are, however, extremely complicated and uncertain. Native speakers can rely on their sense of what is normal and what is not.

V with a coordination structure modifying the verb headword

$$V \leftarrow (^{1/1} M c M ^{1/1})$$

ran (fast and silently)

spent (with increasing recklessness and without consideration for his family)

V with an included nuclear sentence modifying the verb headword

$$V \leftarrow (^1 i |^1 S^1| \quad |^1 V^1|^1)$$

hesitated (when he came)

is succeeding (since he understands the principles involved) left (after he inquired for his wife)

had hesitated (because he wanted more money)

You should notice that included nuclear sentences having functional includers (i_N) can not be used to modify a verb headword.

V with a predicate structure modifying the verb headword

$$V \leftarrow (^1|^1\text{"to"}V_1{}^1| \quad |^1O_2{}^1|^1)$$

worked (to provide   an education for her son)

hastened (to get   a newspaper)

writes (to get   him   a new job)

It is noticeable that "to" $-V_1$ is the usual V of this predicate structure. The V_3 forms are less used, but sometimes occur as in the following example.

The man drowned (trying   to reach shore).

V with a headword structure modifying the verb headword

$$V \leftarrow (\ ^1 M \rightarrow M \rightarrow M \ ^1\ )$$

drove (quite unnecessarily fast)

planted (extremely early in the season)

planned (rather surprisingly well)

Headword structures that modify V always have an M for a headword.

V with auxiliary verbs

As has been noted above, the combination in a multi-word verb of auxiliary verbs with a lexical verb is a headword structure with the lexical verb acting as the headword. The auxiliaries serve as modifiers in regard to time, manner or attitude as illustrated in the following examples.

will come (time)

kept going (manner)

ought to run (attitude)

1. Write as many sentences as your instructor requires to illustrate the various syntax structures that modify a verb headword. Underline the verb and its modifiers, and divide each sentence into its major parts, labeling the parts.
2. Write sentences that have a V consisting of a verb, a single-word modifier and a preposition structure. By shifting the two modifiers to other places in the sentence, find out how many different normal sentences may be made. (A "normal sentence" is one that you yourself would either say or write.)

DISTRIBUTION OF SYNTAX STRUCTURES AS C

Like the other elements in nuclear sentences the C's may consist of syntax structures of various kinds. The following sentences illustrate most of the normal possibilities.

Headword structures as C in nuclear sentence C

```
   S      V          C
|She|  |was|   |very pretty|.
    S       V                C
|They|  |were|   |alone for over two hours|.
  S     V            C
|He|  |is|   |likely to be elected|.
          S            V                    C
|The weather|  |was|   |fine after they got under way|.
        S          V                    C
|The book|  |was|   |very nearly complete by the first of June|.
  S     V              C
|He|  |was|   |quite happy to choose his prize|.
```

All the syntax structures–except non-included nuclear sentences–may be used to combine with an M headword to form a C.

Coordination structures as C in nuclear sentence C

This structure is the only other one that freely acts as C. Its parts consist always of M's or of headword structures with M headwords. Examples are:

```
        S        V          C
   |The girl|  |was|  |tall and slender|.
        S        V                  C
   |The decision|  |was|  |quite clear but bad in its effect|.
          S         V            C
   |Both contestants|  |were|  |either tired or weak|.
```

Headword structures as C in nuclear sentence A–3

```
    S       V       O₂               C
  |We|  |thought|  |him|  |very successful in business|.
    S       V       O₂            C
  |He|  |made|  |that dog|  |very skillful at doing tricks|.
          S         V        O₂              C
  |Schoolteachers|  |make|  |little boys|  |unhappy because they insist
                                                       on quiet|.
```

Coordination structures as C in nuclear sentence A–3

```
     S       V      O₂           C
  |This|  |made|  |her|  |proud and happy|.
       S         V          O₂              C
  |The writers|  |called|  |the shortstop|  |rather small but quick as
                                                        a cat|.
```

• EXERCISE

Write sentences illustrating the use of headword structures and coordination structures as C in both nuclear sentence C and nuclear sentence A 3.

CONCLUSION

The examples given above demonstrate how syntax structures of various kinds may take the place of the parts of other syntax structures. You should notice that non-included nuclear sentences can not be part of any structures other than coordination structures. The joining of two or more non-included nuclear sentences is very common in English speech and writing. Such a sentence as *They wanted higher wages, but they settled for some fringe benefits* illustrates this kind of coordination structure. (This sort of sentence is called a compound sentence.) All other nuclear sentences that are part of other structures must be included nuclear sentences. But the picture presented by these examples is oversimple. This is because any N, V or M may be represented by a structure, whether the N, V or M is or is not an element in the basic structure of the sentence. Let us look at a sentence taken from the writing of a great English author, Cardinal Newman, to see what complications arise in a relatively short sentence.

> Now this is what some great men are very slow to allow; they insist that Education should be confined to some particular and narrow end, and should issue in some definite work, which can be weighed and measured.

The first and most obvious feature of this sentence is that there are two non-included nuclear sentences. Though the two structures do not have a coordinator between them, simply a semicolon, they very well might have an *and,* a *but* or a *for* in place of the semicolon. Thus the sentence is in itself a coordination structure.

Let us now take each nuclear sentence that is non-included and inspect it in turn. We notice that in the structure *Now this is what some great men are very slow to allow* we apparently have a nuclear sentence C. The S is *this,* the V is *is* and the C is the remainder of the structure. But the C begins with a word that is in our list of includers and thus we look for an included nuclear sentence. This included nuclear sentence apparently substitutes for C. Referring to the examples earlier in this chapter we find that this is a normal arrangement. Therefore we can divide the structure and label its parts thus:

S   V   C
|This| |is| |what some great men are very slow to allow|.

Now has been omitted. We may call *now* a sentence modifier and include it in brackets. We have thus accounted for all the elements in the basic structure. But the C is a complicated structure also, which includes, we recognize, an S and a V, a headword structure and some other features that can not be accounted for until we have studied transformations in a later chapter. But we certainly can recognize another nuclear sentence C with a C (*slow*), which is modified by both *very* and *to allow*. Again referring to the examples in this chapter we find that this is normal. Besides *some great men* is clearly a headword structure. We see then that in these eleven words we can find the following structures:

> A non-included nuclear sentence C
> An included nuclear sentence C
> A headword structure with noun headword
> A headword structure with modifier headword
> A predicate structure that we can not yet analyze
> (It includes the words "what" and "to allow.")

The analysis could be carried on into the somewhat more complicated second non-included nuclear sentence, but it is likely that the point has been made: structures are as common as single words in composing the non-included nuclear sentences that are the most distinguishing feature of written English sentences.

• EXERCISE

Inspect the following sentences, also from Newman, and list all the structures you can find by inspection. Compare your list with the examples given in this chapter. In your list record the words that compose the structure and write down the name of the structure, e.g., "included nuclear sentence," "headword structure with noun headword." If you cannot name a group of words that seem to you to be a structure, write the words down and put a question mark beside them.

The ordinary and predominant tendency of good is towards more good.

But waiving the objections to this scheme of ethics, it does not at all get rid of the difficulty.

He has the repose of a mind which lives in itself, while it lives in the world, and which has resources for its happiness when it cannot go abroad.

I say that a cultivated intellect, because it is a good in itself, brings with it a power and a grace to every work and occupation which it undertakes, and enables us to be more useful. . . .

Today I have confined myself to saying that the training of the intellect, which is best for the individual himself, best enables him to discharge his duties to society.

CHAPTER IX

Generating and Analyzing
Syntax Structures

In the preceding chapters we have examined all the units that either by themselves or in combination with other units make sentences. Sentences in speech are always marked by final junctures, you will remember, and sentences in writing are marked by symbols that stand for these final junctures, though in truth the symbols do not *always* stand for final junctures. We have noticed that under the proper conditions each word in the language and each multi-word unit in the language may be a speech sentence, but that writing which is not imitating speech limits itself for the most part to sentences that contain the nuclear sentences described in Chapter IV. The other units, single-word or multi-word, appear almost always as parts of nuclear sentences or as modifiers either of parts of nuclear sentences or of whole nuclear sentences.

We have identified in addition to the nuclear sentence the five classes of multi-word syntax structures and the two classes of words by various pieces of evidence, the principal evidence being the distribution of the units. Other supplementary evidence has been noted, such as the presence of a word in a list and the existence of what are called the inflections of words. In identifying these eight classes we have relied on our own knowledge of English, which, we have learned, is extensive if not very systematic. We have also particularly relied on what looks (or sounds) natural, because as users of the language for a considerable number of years we have discovered by trial and error that some combinations of phonemes or their written counterparts are useful in getting appropriate responses and some are not. Through years of practice we have become so expert that we usually do not consciously plan in advance what we are going to say or write but respond almost immediately and automatically with appropriate sounds or written symbols to the situation we are in. If we have studied a foreign language we have noticed how differently we must act in trying to make sentences. Suppose that we know nothing about French and that we want to write the French equivalent of *That boy is his sister's friend.* We have a French-English dictionary and a French grammar. As speakers of English we recognize that *that boy* is a head-word structure with *boy* as headword. We assume that French may have a similar unit. So we use our dictionary to find the word for *boy.* It turns out to be *garçon.* Now we must find the equivalent for *that.* We look again at the dictionary, which tells us that there are four possibilities—*ce, cet, cette, ces.* Only the first two are masculine and singular, and after confirming that *garçon* is also masculine and singular we must select between them. We have recourse to the grammar and soon discover that *cet* comes only before vowel sounds. We thus have *ce garçon* as our final choice.

Now we notice that in our nomenclature *ce garçon* is an S. We know enough about language to know that an S often has a special form different from O_2, O_1 or C, but our French grammar doesn't say anything about any form changes of this sort in regard to nouns. We assume, therefore, that *ce garçon* will be appropriate.

The next word is the verb. We choose to look *be* up in the grammar, which, we hope, will furnish us with a paradigm. It does, and we discover that the corresponding French form to *is* is *est,* and that there seems to be no selection problem involved. Now we have *ce garçon est.*

Once more looking at the English sentence, we recognize a second headword structure, which is C and which has *friend* for its headword. We will start with *friend.* The dictionary gives us the word *ami.* We must then check the grammar to find if *ami* has a special form when it is C. We do not find that it has, so we make no change. We now notice that the formula for *his sister's friend* is $M \rightarrow M_N \rightarrow N$; thus $M \rightarrow M_N$ is also a modification structure with M_N as the headword. We now look up *sister* and find *soeur.* But the form we need is the equivalent of the English genitive. We try the grammar, once more, to find that in French the genitive is made by using the preposition *de* plus the plain form of the noun. We write *de soeur ami*. This leaves us with only *his* to deal with. This word again requires us to make a choice, this time between *son, sa, ses*. We choose *sa* because the grammar tells us that the personal pronoun agrees with what it modifies in number and gender. Now our sentence is complete. *Ce garçon est sa de soeur ami.* And we might leave it at that unless we wonder about word order. If we investigate the problem of word order we discover that while SVC is appropriate in French, the order within the C is quite unnatural. The *de soeur* must follow *ami,* the *sa* should, as in English, come between the preposition *de* and the N_{pr}; *ami,* thus left alone, should have an *l'* added. These discoveries require several minutes' work. And we finally come up with a French sentence that a Frenchman would think made sense. *Ce garçon est l'ami de sa soeur.*

What we have done is to generate a sentence. This means that in response to a particular situation or previous utterance we have selected certain symbols from a large number available, we have organized the symbols in units and we have arranged the units in a certain order. And always we have been required by the language to select a particular symbol because of our previous selection. When we want to make S equivalent to *that boy,* we must select *garçon* rather than *garçons* and we must select *ce* rather than *cet, cette* or *ces*. We would have been laughed at or corrected had we put down *cette garçons*. What is more, we might not have been understood and thus might have been given a response inappropriate to the meaning we intended.

The process just described in perhaps tedious detail is a process that we accomplish in English at almost lightning speed day after day quite unconsciously. The ability to select instantaneously the appropriate sounds, syntax units and word order combined with intonation is perhaps the greatest human accomplishment. Yet we treat it lightly. It is, we think, remarkable when we are left speechless, and we mention the fact. However, we do not frequently find it important to mention the fact that we spoke, for speaking we always expect to be able to do.

Certainly one of the functions of grammar should be to describe the process by which the syntax units of a language are generated or put together. Of course a complete statement of this process would be immensely complicated and consequently impossible here. But a few examples can be given, and further exploration can be made by anyone interested. It is necessary in devising possible statements for describing the generation of units to be very careful not to include any statements that could lead to impossible or unnatural structures. The two things that one must be careful about are, therefore, to include all the possibilities and not to include any structures that are impossible in English.

Let us start with a simple situation in which we will imagine oral discourse is used. A person says to another, *Where is the book about insects?* An appropriate response would be *In the bookcase.* What are the conditions required for generating this response?

First of all there are a large number of possible responses, which may be organized roughly into the following classes:

statement	In the bookcase
	I don't know
	I think it's been returned
question	Huh?
	Why do you want it?
	Did you look in the bookcase?
exclamation	Forget it!
non-language	A shrug
	A grunt
	Complete silence without body motion

The illustrations possible above are only samples; of course there are many other responses in each of the classes. And also notice that the classes are overlapping in meaning. For instance, *Did you look in the bookcase?* is quite similar in meaning to *I think it's in the bookcase.* The problem of why one of these two similar statements should be chosen rather than the other is very complex and cannot be examined here. It depends on the relationship of the persons involved and on the speaker's physiological and psychological condition, as well as on the physical context. It is sufficient for our purposes to note that from a large number of possibilities one particular form of response is selected. From this large number of possibilities we actually do select instantaneously and quite without effort a structure beginning with *in*. When we have made the sounds /*in*/ we have in effect chosen a preposition structure. All we can do is to go ahead with the rest of it, unless of course we want to stop and start again. Therefore once the decision to respond with a structure beginning with a preposition is made, the die is cast, the limitations on the possible choices become operative.

First, a noun or a noun substitute is the only unit that may follow *in*. The selection is limited then to these classes. If we present the structure in a formula it will be S ⟶ pr N_{pr}. The pr is *in*, and out of the possibilities for what is to follow the preposition—that is, a noun or noun substitute—one is selected. These possibilities are

N (singular or plural)	—	in hope
N_p	—	in mine
N (genitive)	—	in Henry's
Headword structure	—	in the bookcase
Predicate structure	—	in writing letters
Included nuclear sentence	—	in what he wanted
Coordination structure	—	in spring and summer

We may also select a marker or a modifier and thus delay the statement of the noun. From the available possibilities we select the word unit *the*. As we know, *the* may be followed by a limited number of words too. Directly after it may normally come one or more modifiers that will eventually lead us to the noun or the noun substitute that forms the headword of the headword structure.

The number of modifiers is theoretically unlimited but practically, as we know from our reading, only four or five at the most normally come between the pr and the headword. In this particular example there are no modifiers except the m. A further decision must be made when the headword is reached. At this point we have completed a unit. Therefore we may stop for a noticeable time and mark this stop by # juncture. But we may also add, for example, multi-word modifiers and possibly a single-word modifier, or we may start a nuclear sentence, either included or non-included. On this occasion we decide to stop and pronounce "bookcase" in a manner that creates a # juncture.

The process just described is very similar to the process of making the French sentence by a non-French-speaking person. Here, in creating *In the bookcase,* the total situation, physical and psychological, corresponds to the English sentence that is to be changed into its French equivalent. The French dictionary and grammar, which we used in order to find the possibilities for the French sentence, correspond to our stock of words (our vocabulary) and to our previously acquired knowledge of word order and word relationship. We select the form of unit to be used and the classes of items to be included within the unit-to-be, as well as the actual vocabulary items (words). We cannot use either a form or an item that we haven't previously learned, though if we are uncertain which of two to select we may hesitate a moment and do a little conscious cogitating, or we may even, when writing, appeal to a dictionary or a grammar book.

• E X E R C I S E

With the help of Chapter VIII and the use of your own knowledge of English, show how the form of the *responses* below is generated. List at each stage all the possibilities you can.

(a) Opening remark: "What are you doing?"
       Response: "Writing a letter."
(b) Opening remark: "What's wrong with you?"
       Response: "Nothing to do."
(c) Opening remark: "He's got a new T-bird."
       Response: "Like mine."

As we know, the nuclear sentences are the normal forms for sentences in written English. They too are generated by selecting from our word stock and by organizing our selection of words according to the system that we have stored in our brains. In the following description we will use a sentence that does not require some previous sentence to which it is a response. Such a statement might be made by a person returning to an inner room after answering a ring of the doorbell.

As a result of the experience he has just undergone, the person utters the word *those*. Normally after the word *those* there may occur silence, a noun, a noun substitute or a verb. The most frequent noun substitute would be of course a headword structure. In this example the physical situation asks for a noun. But the grammatical situation makes a limitation. After *those* one can find only a plural noun. *Men* fits both the physical and the grammatical situation. *Those men* can be followed by various kinds of units as well as by silence. The physical situation determines whether there will be silence or not and also selects one from the possibilities that the grammatical situation will allow. Among the more likely possibilities are: modifiers of *men,* a V, a v, a modifier of a V that will follow, a sentence modifier, a coordinator. Let's try some samples.

Those men *at the door*	(modifier of men)
Those men *who rang the bell*	(modifier of men)
Those men *wanted* (or *want*)	(verb)
Those men *must*	(auxiliary verb)
Those men *suddenly*	(modifier of a verb that is to follow)
Those men, *naturally,*	(sentence modifier)
Those men *and*	(coordinator)

Out of this variety of possibilities (and there may be others) the particular situation demands a V. The grammatical situation limits the possible forms of the V to those forms that appear in column 1 or column 4 of the verb paradigm. Again from these two possibilities the situation requires the column 4 form of *want*.

We now have: *those men wanted.* This is, in form, a nuclear sentence B. But it doesn't have to remain a nuclear sentence B. And if it does so remain we can add one or more modifiers to the V and, following them, sentence modifiers. However, the situation demands an O_2. Without listing all the possibilities for O_2, we can say that in this situation *my* is the next word added, and *signature,* a noun, follows to complete a nuclear sentence A 1. At this point, too, one of the three final junctures *may* occur, but of course obviously it need not. Additional modifiers, coordinators, prepositions, includers could follow. But for the speaker in this situation a satisfactory place for a stop has occurred. A # juncture is made, and the sentence ends. The sentence would be expressed by this formula:

$$|{}^1\text{M N}^1| \quad |{}^1\text{V}_4{}^1| \quad |{}^1\text{m N}^1|$$

The two accounts of forming sentences just given describe in a very crude way how our personal computer (our brain) works. Stored within it are a large number of vocabulary items (words) and also a series of grammatical principles. You may call the grammatical principles generalizations or rules if you wish. When we ask our brain a question, which is always *How do I respond by language to this situation?*, the brain immediately responds by doing two things with great rapidity. It selects appropriate words and it puts these words together in whatever way the grammatical system that we use permits. For some of us it arranges *he* and *done* and *it* in the system (the structure) *He done it.* For still others the brain has to select between *done* and *did* for this structure. In our normal day-to-day activities these actions of our brain pass unnoticed. We are simply aware of the finished product, the utterance. But when we sit down to compose on paper, the automatic controls often do not work. We must consciously push all the buttons, throw all the switches, undo what we've done, start again and so on. In other words we must think about what we are going to write. And that this is true makes clear one of the major differences between speaking and writing. Speaking, unless we are making a speech, is almost always spontaneous; writing is more often than not deliberate and is almost always changed in some ways as a result of second thoughts.

The sentence *Those men wanted my signature* is a complete nuclear sentence. As we know, the nuclear sentence is one of five possible nuclear sentences. The five have from two to four units, or elements, separated in our formulas by vertical lines. In addition to these elements that form nuclear sentences a written sentence may include one or more sentence modifiers. In the sentence *When father got home he ate dinner with the family* we notice two nuclear sentences, one of which is preceded by a word from the list of pure includers. This one is therefore a modifier, but not of *he*. Thus it is a sentence modifier, for we have defined sentence modifiers as those modifiers that do not modify a word next to them. Also the unit starting with *with* is a preposition structure that most people would agree does not modify *dinner,* and thus is a sentence modifier. The generalized formula for this sentence would be

$$S \longrightarrow [^1M^1] \quad |^1S^1| \quad |^1V^1| \quad |^1O_2{}^1| \quad [^2M^2]$$

Written sentences are almost always composed of a nuclear sentence either with or without sentence modifiers. A diligent examination of current professional writing will turn up only a few sentences that do not contain at least one non-included nuclear sentence.

• EXERCISES

1. Examine 100 sentences in a current magazine and count the sentences that do not contain a non-included nuclear sentence. Sentences that profess to reproduce speech should not be included. List all the sentences you find without non-included nuclear sentences and determine what syntax structure is being used as a sentence.
2. Show how normal written sentences may be generated by starting with the following units. (The sentences should be non-question.)

When	Suddenly
Above	What we need
That	In the morning
Richard	To succeed
Traveling	Walking the dog
The	And
Pretty	Who

3. What classes of words or units can serve as the S for the verb *makes?* As a result of your investigation can you make a generalization (a rule) for the S of verbs like *makes,* i.e., V_2 verbs?
4. If *He will* is written as the beginning of a piece of writing without quotation marks, what must follow sooner or later?
5. Organize the following list of words and structures into a single sentence using only one class of function words.

the suburbs	the branches
my house	the trees
dawn	sing
no birds	

By the process of building sentences we may learn another very important truth about the system of English. This truth is that when we add to a basic structure modifiers of various kinds we are adding elements that could be expressed as non-included nuclear sentences.

Let us start with a simple nuclear sentence and add a series of modifiers of various kinds. The nuclear sentence we shall start with is:

John wrote a letter

The generalized formula for this sentence is $|^1S^1|$ $|^1V^1|$ $|^1O_2{}^1|$. This means it is a nuclear sentence A 1. Its specific formula is $|^1N^1|$ $|^1V_4{}^1|$ $|^1m\,N^1|$. For *John* we can easily substitute a headword structure such as *My brother John*. The formula for the sentence becomes $|^1m\,M_n\,N^1|$ $|^1V_4{}^1|$ $|^1m\,N^1|$. Now we can add an included nuclear sentence such as *who lives in Pennsylvania and is a lawyer.* The sentence will then be symbolized as

$$|^1m\,M_N N \leftarrow (^1\ |^2i_N{}^2|\ \ |^2/^1V_2 \leftarrow (^2pr\,N_{pr}{}^2)\ c\ V_2\ ^1/^2|\ \ |^2m\,N^2|\ ^1)\ ^1|$$
$$|^1V_4{}^1|\ \ ^1m\,N^1|$$

We may also add to the other two basic elements, the V and the O_2. For example we might add *impulsively* to V_4 making the structure $M_{AV} \rightarrow V_4$. And we might add to O_2 such structures as *to his Congress-*

man (^{3}pr m̲ N$_{pr}$ ^{3}) and *supporting the bill to aid education* (^{4} |^{3}V$_3$^{3}|
|^{3}m N ← $\overline{(^5 |^4 \text{“to”} V_1{}^4|}$ |^{4}N^4| ^{5}) ^{4}).

Now the formula for the whole sentence would look like this:

|^{1}m M$_N$ N ← (^{1} |^2 i$_N$ ^{2}| |^2/^{1} V$_2$ ← (^{2} pr N$_{pr}$ ^{2}) c V$_2$ ^{1}/^{2}| |^{2}m N^2|^2)^1|
|^{1}M$_{AV}$ → V$_4$^{1}| |^{1}m N $\overleftarrow{← (^3 \text{pr m N}_{pr}{}^3)}$ (^{4} |^{3}V$_3$^{3}| |^3 m N ← (^{5} |^4 “to”
V$_1$ ^{4}| |^{4}N^4| ^{5}) ^{3}|^4) ^{1}|

By substituting various structures for the single words, that is, by
adding modifiers we have evolved a fairly complex sentence:

> My brother John, who lives in Pennsylvania and is a lawyer,
> impulsively wrote a letter to his Congressman supporting the
> bill to aid education.

We have changed a sentence of four words to a sentence of twenty-
four words by adding modifiers. But we have not changed in any way
the original structure. We have simply slipped into the place of the
simple and less precise elements more complicated and more precise
structures.

We must realize that every time we add a modifier we are adding
a meaning unit that could be expressed as a nuclear sentence. Let us
work through our sentence. S in the original sentence is *John*. We
added *my brother* first. Here are two modifiers (one is a marker), that
could be expressed as *He is a brother* and *He is mine*. Then we added
who lives in Pennsylvania and is a lawyer. This could be expressed
in the nuclear sentences:

> He is alive.
> Pennsylvania is his home.
> He is a lawyer.

To the V$_4$ we added *impulsively*. This can be expressed by:

> He was impulsive.

To the O$_2$ we added *to his Congressman*. This can be expressed by:

> His Congressman was the addressee of the letter.

Then we added *supporting the bill to aid education:*

> The letter supported the bill.
> The bill will aid education.

Putting these structures in order we have:

> John wrote a letter.
> He is a brother.
> He is mine.
> He is alive.
> Pennsylvania is his home.
> He is a lawyer.
> He was impulsive.
> His Congressman was the addressee of the letter.
> The letter supported a bill.
> The bill will aid education.

These ten sentences are comprised of forty-three words, almost twice the number in the final sentence developed.

Again we can only marvel at the collective ingenuity of the language-makers who through many years of trial and error have developed a system in which the number of words needed to symbolize a fairly complicated series of events is kept far fewer than would be necessary to express each event separately. And of course this is done by developing structures that can substitute for the parts of complete nuclear structures and that will equally well communicate the necessary information. You will notice too that once we know the system we feel that the communication is more successful in the form of the single sentence than it is by using the ten separate sentences.

Further, growing out of this concept is a more precise definition of "modification." To modify was defined earlier as "to make some concept more precise," and a modifier was defined as a word or a structure that made more precise and specific another word or structure. Now it is possible to say that modification is the act of changing potential nuclear sentences to other syntax structures or to single words in order to reduce the number of words required to express a complex series of events.

Reduce to modifiers as many as possible of the following groups of non-included nuclear sentences. (The nuclear sentences are in the order in which the modifiers appear in the original sentences, and the basic nuclear sentence is marked with a *.)

> a. I picked out books. * (the V is "picked out")
> The number was indefinite.
> The library contained the books.
> I filled a shelf.
> The closet contained the shelf.
> She gave me a possession.
> My possession was the closet.
> b. My papers lay. *
> They are buried.
> The rosebush covers them.
> c. A time elapsed.
> The time was long.
> He walked. *
> I walked.
> We were together.
> He bragged.
> His bragging concerned his love.
> His bragging concerned his honor.

CHAPTER X

Transformations of Syntax Structures

Up to this point we have concerned ourselves only with the kind of sentence illustrated by the three basic nuclear sentences. Though these have been expanded by replacing single-word elements with multi-word elements, the basic structure has always been one of the structures displayed in Chapter IV. Most people would, in their own writing, however, feel uncomfortable if they were limited to the three basic structures in their sentences. For there are a considerable number of departures from the norm of these structures, and there is always the possibility of developing more. One of the most interesting of word games is to experiment with re-arranging the available sentence elements in order to gain new accuracy of meaning, new piquancy of expression, without harming the basic concept to be communicated or rendering the sentence unintelligible.

Some of the re-arrangements and changes are so frequent that they are normal. Everyone knows, for example, that a sentence such as *John is my brother* can be changed into a different kind of sentence by changing the order of *John* and *is*, which results in *Is John my brother?* Simply by reversing the positions of *John* and *is*, we create an entirely new sentence but we do not change the meaning of the individual words.

You will notice of course that we started with a regular nuclear sentence C. This we may call the "base-form." Then we changed the position of the first two words. This transformed the meaning from statement to question. The resulting sentence we call a "transformation." You must remember that all transformations of written sentences are based on one of the five nuclear sentences. Therefore, a transformation of a sentence is a re-arrangement of a base-form with or without the addition of function words or changes of inflection. But none of the elements of the base-form are removed and no additional structural elements are added. A transformation of nuclear sentence A 2 must have the four elements of the base-form and no more or less. The results of transformations are various. Sometimes emphasis is gained, that is, stresses are readjusted. Sometimes a different kind of response is elicited. Sometimes a statement is denied. Everybody uses transformations regularly, and there is a system of transformation that we call regular.

Besides these regular transformations with which almost all users of English are familiar, there are others that appear infrequently and that are distinctly odd. Browning, for example, in a line of poetry says: *Irks care the crop-filled bird?* This strikes nearly all readers as odd, though if we know the meaning of *irk* and thus classify it properly as a verb there is no real difficulty in understanding. But if we did not know how *irk* usually was classified, we should really be in trouble, because *irks care* is possible as S V or a V S, as far as form and word order are concerned. We are also helped to understand by the analogy of another verb or two. For instance we can say *Has he a lot of money?* or *Is John that new man's name?* Thus the oddness gives a certain interesting quality to the sentence without damaging the communication—at least with the sort of readers Browning was addressing. The danger of going to a point where the reader will not be able to notice the clues to meaning is always present of course. Had Browning written *Irks the crop-full bird care* he would have made a greater difficulty for the reader, though even this is not without clues as to the relation of the elements.

We make a transformation by using one or more of three devices, which are

(1) changing the word order
(2) adding or changing inflectional morphemes
(3) adding function words that have a minimum of lexical meaning.

The first device has already been illustrated. The second and third devices (as well as the first) may be illustrated by the passive transformation. Starting with *The policeman chases the thief,* we can write this sentence *The thief is chased by the policeman.* You will notice that the words *the, policeman, the* and *thief* have not been changed in any way except position. *Chases,* on the contrary, has the allomorph /iz/ replaced by the allomorph /t/. Moreover, the function word *is* has been added (in a certain prescribed position) and the function word *by* has been inserted (also in a particular position). Notice that all three of the devices are essential if we are to get the proper information communicated. There are no shortcuts. The order of words must be changed, the inflectional morphemes must be changed and the function word *by* must be added. Failure to do any of these prevents the transformed sentence from making sense.

Transformations enable us to get different effects and responses from the same set of words. An example of this change in effect is seen in a particular sort of question transformation. Given as a starting structure *Boys ride bicycles,* we may make a question transformation by rewriting it *Do boys ride bicycles?* We may also rewrite it *Boys ride bicycles, don't they?* Naturally there is a considerable difference in effect between the base and the question transformation, but presumably there is also some difference between the two forms of the question. What it is, is difficult to perceive, but since we sometimes use one and sometimes the other, it seems reasonable to suppose that we choose on the basis of the responses expected or hoped for. We must therefore have some kind of reason for using one rather than the other. The successful use of transformations gives to writing a distinctive, individual style and contributes to the success of communication.

More transformations can be made of nuclear sentences, either non-included or included, than of the other four structures, but some transformations can be made of all. We shall start with the normal transformations of non-included nuclear sentences. No attempt will be made to illustrate all possible transformations, because expert users of the language have devised many odd and infrequent transformations in order to get what they hope will be special effects.

Each non-included nuclear sentence will be discussed in turn, though the transformations of all five have a good deal in common. The symbol "T" will be used for transformations, "T-question" meaning "the transformation for questions." The starting point for all transformations will be the form of the structure described in Chapter IV. A heavy arrow (~~➤) will be used to mean "is to be expressed as." Thus "~~➤ T-passive" means "is to be expressed as the passive transformation."

TRANSFORMATIONS OF NUCLEAR SENTENCE A 1

The normal transformations of A 1 are "negative," "question," "imperative," "passive," "emphasis" and "it." All nuclear sentences A 1 can be transformed for negative, question, passive and emphasis, but only one type of base form can be transformed for imperative and normally the "it" transformation requires special types of subjects.

Negative transformation

The two function words *not* and *never* are essential in this transformation. *Not* can only be used by itself in an A 1 sentence in modern English with a multi-word verb. Consequently, if the base form contains only a single-word V, an auxiliary must be supplied. This v is always *do, does* or *did,* whichever is appropriate to the sentence. This has no meaning at all; it simply makes it possible to use *not.* As a result of adding *do, does* or *did,* the V must always be V_1 in a T-negative using *not.* Examples:

> The boys ride their bicycles. ~~➤ The boys *do not (don't)* ride their bicycles.
> That little boy hit the ball well. ~~➤ That little boy *does not (doesn't)* hit the ball well.
> The Democrats planned their campaign with great skill. ~~➤ The Democrats *did not (didn't)* plan their campaign with great skill.

Notice: (1) We have a choice between *do not* and *don't,* between *does not* and *doesn't* and between *did not* and *didn't.* In writing we often use the two-word form, in speaking usually the contracted form. (2) The *not* always comes between the v and the V. If there are two or more v's, the *not* always comes after the first one. This is true of all multi-word verbs, not only when the auxiliary is *do, does* or *did*. *He has been getting the local paper.* ⟶ *He has not been getting the local paper.* (3) If the base form has *some* as an O_2 or as an M of the O_2, the transformation requires this to be replaced by *any*. *He wants some breakfast* ⟶ *He doesn't want any breakfast.*

Never can be used with both single-word and multi-word verbs. Moreover its position is not fixed as is the position of *not*. Examples:

That man rides the bus. ⟶ That man *never* rides the bus.
He will get a new car.   ⟶ He *will never* get a new car.
also   ⟶ He *never will* get a new car.

Notice: (1) Only certain sorts of base structures may use *never* in T-negatives. For instance: *That man rides the bus every day* is written as *That man does not ride the bus every day*, not *That man never rides the bus every day*. The reason for this situation is that *never* involves time and if some other word or words involving time are in the sentence a conflict may result. (2) A less important transformation pattern with *never* involves a change in word order. *He will get a larger salary* → *Never will he get a larger salary*. Here the first v and the S change positions, and when the V is a single word, *do, does* or *did* must be added. This T-negative sounds a little formal or perhaps old-fashioned, but it is not uncommon. (3) The position of *never* is generally just before or just after the first v. If there is only a V *never* normally comes just before it. Other positions are abnormal.

Sentences that use *no* are not to be considered T-negative. *He has no problems* has an O_2 consisting of a noun and a modifier; *no* is equivalent to such a word as *some* in *He has some problems.*

Question transformation

There are several ways of making questions from nuclear sentence A 1. The simplest is to change from a # juncture to a || juncture, leaving the rest of the sentence as it is. It is only in this type of sentence that the question mark is useful. It tells you what juncture to end this sentence with. In all other question sentences, a question signal appears early in the sentence—usually it is the first word. The question signallers are

(1) an auxiliary verb followed by the subject. Examples:

> Has he written that letter?
> Will they buy the house?
> May I ask a question?
> Does the baby like cereal?

(2) an interrogator, which may be *why, where, when, how, what, who, whom, which* or a preposition structure with the N_{pr} *who* (not frequent in writing), *whom, whose, which* or *what* coming as the first element in the sentence. Examples:

What do you have?
Why are you doing that?
Whom did you meet? (In speech this would probably be *Who did you meet?*)
From whom did you ask permission?
For what would you sacrifice your comfort?

(3) by adding to the sentence an auxiliary verb plus *not* plus the pronoun that is appropriate to the subject of the base sentence. Examples:

> Bob has got a new job, hasn't he?
> An atom bomb will destroy a city, won't it?
> Young men ought to play outdoor games, oughtn't they?

Notice: (1) Since the first of these three transformations requires starting the structure with a v, we must supply one if the sentence has only a V. This supplied v is *do, does* or *did. Mary had a little lamb* ⟶ *Did Mary have a little lamb?* One verb does not always require supplying a v. It is *have.* We may start with *He has time to do it?* This may be transformed to *Has he time to do it?* or *Does he have time to do it?* The second is more common. (2) The questions started with interrogators must be separated into two classes: (a) those that start with pure interrogators and (b) those that start with functional interrogators. The transformations involving interrogators will be considered as a unit later in the chapter. (3) Questions with the question signal coming at the end as in *He saw the bird, didn't he?* or *They have found the child, haven't they?* also require an auxiliary verb. Thus *do, does* and *did* must be supplied if no v is in the base sentence. The use of the contracted form of the negative word *not* (n't) requires the word order illustrated, i.e., v "n't" N_p; if the full form of *not* is used, the word order is v N_p "not"? as in *They were entering the contest reluctantly, were they not?* Occasionally the subject of the principal nuclear sentence will be repeated instead of the appropriate pronoun. This is most familiar in talking to little children, i.e., *Jimmy ate all his meal like a big boy, didn't Jimmy?* This almost never shows up in writing. The question signal discussed immediately above is to be considered a sentence modifier, therefore to be enclosed in brackets in all formulas.

Imperative transformation

Transformations for imperative can be made from only one kind of nuclear sentence A 1. The base form must have *you* as S, and V_1 as V or v. The O_2 can be any appropriate word or structure. The imperative is made by dropping the S. Examples:

You make the salad. ⟶ Make the salad.
You get what you want. ⟶ Get what you want.
You enjoy getting your hair cut. ⟶ Enjoy getting your hair cut.
You do like it. ⟶ Do like it.

Notice: The word imperative applied to this transformation should not be thought of as signifying any thing in particular about the nature of the sentence meaning. It simply names the transformation that results when this particular type of base sentence is treated in this way, i.e., by dropping the subject.

As so often happens, the verb *be* has a peculiarity in this transformation. We sometimes find an auxiliary verb at the beginning of a T-imperative, such as *Keep trying the door.* Of course this sentence uses the V_1 form of the auxiliary. But in sentences using *be* as an auxiliary we start as is normal with a sentence like *You are keeping score.* If we drop the *you* we get an impossible sentence because the V_1 form of *be* is not used with *you* in a nuclear sentence. Instead we use a V_2 form. Since imperatives never use anything but V_1 forms, we must substitute *be* for *are.* The resulting imperative is, therefore, *be keeping score.* (This has led to the use of *be* with *you* in the base structure, as in *You be keeping score while I go for a hot dog.*) Naturally this variant in the T-imperative is more important in the transformations of nuclear sentence C, where the verb is very frequently *be.*

Passive transformation

The passive transformation is a feature of those nuclear sentences that have O_2. It is a device for putting O_2 in front of the V and the S behind the V (or even for omitting the subject completely). This is accomplished by the use of function words and inflection changes. The function words are the auxiliary verbs *be* and *get* and the preposition *by.* Examples:

Most people want three meals a day. ⟶
Three meals a day are wanted by most people.
The policeman will catch the burglars. ⟶
The burglars will get caught by the policeman.
Somebody noticed it. ⟶
It was noticed.
They devised a new plan. ⟶
A new plan was devised by them.

Notice: (1) The O_2 of the base sentence is moved to the left of the V. (If the O_2 is a pronoun a form change may occur.) (2) The appropriate form of the v is determined by whether the O_2 is singular or plural and by the tense of the verb in the base sentence. Example:

He has beaten them. ⟶ They have been beaten by him.
$$|^1S^1|\quad |^1{}_{V_2}\,V_5{}^1|\quad |^1O_2{}^1| \longrightarrow |^1O_2{}^1|\quad |^1\,{}_{V_1}\,{}_{V_5}\,V_5 \leftarrow (\text{``by''}\ S)\,^1|$$

The v which comes next before the V must be a form of *be* or *get.* The V must always be a V_5. The S becomes the N_{pr} in a preposition structure modifying V_5. And if the S is a pronoun with a special N_{pr} form, it must have this form.

> The soldiers had disobeyed their officers. ⟶
> The officers had been disobeyed by the soldiers.
> They punished him severely. ⟶
> He was punished severely by them.
> (Notice the change of form in *they* and *him*.)

(3) The ("by" N_{pr}) is often omitted, especially when the subject of the base sentence is vague or easily understood from context, or when the writer does not wish to use the word that would be the subject of the base sentence. A base sentence such as *Someone whom I don't want to name reported these facts to me* is often written in T-passive as *These facts were reported to me*. Or one such as *You will notice the absence of commas* will be written as *The absence of commas will be noticed*. Or one such as *Someone (I don't know who) wrote the letter to me* will be written *The letter was written to me*. In order to show in a formula that the ("by" N_{pr}) is not required in all T-passives, the symbol $\pm$ is used in front of it. Thus the T-passive general formula is $|^1O_2{}^1|$ $|^1$ "$\overset{\text{"be"}}{\text{get}}$" $V_5 \pm \leftarrow$ ("by" N_{pr}) ^{1}. (4) You will notice that the T-passive made from nuclear sentence A 1 is very much like nuclear sentence B in having only two essential structural parts, the S from the base sentence having become a modifier.

Emphasis transformation

The T-emphasis resembles the passive in that it brings the O_2 of the base sentence from behind the V to the position in front of the V. This T is by no means so common as the passive, and many people never use it. It has, however, been used frequently enough to justify its inclusion here. In essence it is a very simple T, the process being simply to move the O_2 in front of the S without making any other changes. Examples:

> They detest their neighbors. ⟶
> Their neighbors they detest.

My professor can read verse well. ⟶
Verse my professor can read well.
I enjoy a little snack and a bottle of beer. ⟶
A little snack and a bottle of beer I enjoy.

Notice: (1) This T, though normal, is not frequent. (2) In speech a conspicuous single-bar juncture (|) occurs between the O_2 and the S. In writing, this juncture may be indicated by a comma, but more frequently the writer relies on the unusual juxtaposition of the O_2 and the S to signal the nature of the structure. As a result if the last word in the O_2 appears to be related to the first word of the S in a more nearly normal way than this structure demands, confusion and ambiguity result and it is inadvisable to employ the T-emphasis. Examples:

Nobody wanted the money. ⟶
The money nobody wanted.
(This might easily be thought of as a headword structure with an included nuclear sentence modifying the noun *money*.)
People need space. ⟶
Space people need.
(*Space* could be taken as a M_N modifying *people*.)

It transformation

The T-it puts the meaningless function word *it* in the normal position of S, while the S is transferred to a position after O_2. The T occurs most frequently when an included nuclear sentence or a predicate structure or a "to" $-V_1$ is the S of the base sentence. Example:

That he should be our sponsor makes sense. ⟶
It makes sense that he should be our sponsor.
To find her alone surprised him. ⟶
It surprised him to find her alone.
To participate pleased my father. ⟶
It pleased my father to participate.

Notice: (1) No change occurs except in word order and the addition of *it*. (2) Since *it* is the only word so used, we write the word itself into the formula, i.e., "it" $|^1V^1|$ $|^1O_2{}^1|$ $|^1S^1|$.

These are the regular, normal transformations of nuclear sentence A 1. The principles stated for these transformations are used for the transformations of other nuclear sentences. Consequently reference will be made in the following pages to the nuclear sentence A 1 transformations.

You recognize of course that the transformations can be used as base structures to make further transformations. The T-negative as a base can be transformed (1) for question, as *We have not received our supplies yet* ⟶ *Haven't we (have we not) received our supplies yet?* or (2) for imperative if the conditions for the base sentence are complied with, as *You do not (don't) expect much money* ⟶ *Don't (do not) expect much money* or (3) for passive, as *Our children don't need that kind of luxury* ⟶ *That kind of luxury isn't (is not) needed by our children* or (4) for emphasis (*He doesn't like oysters* ⟶ *Oysters he doesn't like*) or (5) for *it* (*To overcome the opposition didn't require a great deal of eoffrt* ⟶ *It didn't require a great deal of effort to overcome the opposition*).

The T-question as base can transform (1) for negative, as *Did you like the show?* ⟶ *Didn't you (did you not) like the show?* (2) for passive (*Did the Reds clobber the Cardinals?* ⟶ *Were the Cardinals clobbered by the Reds?*) (3) for *it* (*Did that he was not chosen hurt him?* ⟶ *Did it hurt him that he was not chosen?*) (The base sentence, of course, would never be used; the transformation always.)

The T-passive as base can transform (1) for negative (*He is supported by his wife* ⟶ *He is not supported by his wife*) (2) for question (*He is supported by his wife* ⟶ *Is he supported by his wife?*) or (*He is supported by his wife, isn't he?*) (3) for imperative (*You are controlled by my experience* ⟶ *Be controlled by my experience*). (Notice that *are*—the present tense form that goes with *you*—is replaced by the V_1 form *be*. This is required in all T-imperatives that involve the verb *be*.)

The T-imperative can transform for negative. (*Write a letter* ⟶ *Don't write a letter*.)

The T-emphasis can be transformed for negative. (*Most people he liked* ⟶ *Most people he didn't like*.)

The T-*it* can be transformed (1) for negative (*It hurt my father*

to give up his plans ➤ *It did not hurt my father to give up his plans*)
or (2) for question (*Did it hurt my father to give up his plans?*).

• EXERCISE

The best way to appreciate the system of the transformation process
is to experiment with it. Thus many exercises in which the various
transformations are used as bases should be done. Starting with the
following sentences as bases, see how many of the five principal
transformations you can make. Then using as a base each transformation you have devised see how many transformations of this
you can make. If you fully explore the possibilities, doing one sentence a day should be sufficient.

a. They broadened the basis of life and intelligence.
b. Christianity substituted for them boundless devotion to that
   pattern of self-conquest.
c. Our ancestors learned that the earth is the center of the
   visible universe.
d. They may not have sufficiently observed another thing.
e. To make an effort to defeat communism requires great cour-
   age and self-sacrifice.
f. Getting more of the good things in life keeps our noses to
   the grindstone.

In doing this kind of exercise it is important that the instructor be
able to tell what you are trying to do. Therefore you should be
very careful to label each base sentence and each transformation
that you are making from that base sentence. Please be sure you
make clear when you change from one base sentence to a different
base sentence.

TRANSFORMATIONS OF NUCLEAR SENTENCE A 2

Since nuclear sentences A 2 and A 3 resemble nuclear sentence A 1,
it is desirable to discuss their transformations next. Most of the

regular transformations are identical with those for nuclear sentence A 1 and may be worked out by the rules already stated. Only the passive and the emphasis transformations require supplementary discussion.

Passive transformation

Like nuclear sentence A 1, nuclear sentence A 2 can transform for passive by changing the verb inflection, adding function words and interchanging S and O_2. For example:

> The crowd gave John three cheers. ⟶
> Three cheers were given John by the crowd.
> In formula form $|^1S^1|$ $|^1O_1{}^1|$ $|^1O_2{}^1|$ ⟶
> $|^1O_2{}^1|$ $|^1\text{"be"} V_5{}^1|$ $|^1O_1{}^1|$ $[\pm \text{"by"} S]$

You will notice, of course, that the O_1 does not change in either form or position and that the "by" S becomes a sentence modifier since it does not modify O_1.

But the T-passive may also be made by changing the position of O_1 instead of O_2. That is: *John was given three cheers by the crowd* is just as good a T-passive as *Three cheers were given John by the crowd*. Notice that the forms of *be* differ in these two versions, for the verb has its form determined by the element immediately at its left whether this be S, O_2 or O_1.

Emphasis transformation

Just as the T-passive may be carried out by moving either O_2 or O_1 to the left of the verb, so may the T-emphasis.

> The stranger handed Michael money. ⟶
> Michael, the stranger handed money. *or*
> Money the stranger handed Michael.

The slight strangeness of these transformations suggests that this type of transformation is probably less frequent with nuclear sentence A 2 than with A 1. And, too, the use of a preposition structure as a sentence modifier at the left of the verb instead of the O_1 is probably more common than the T-passive, i.e., *To Michael the stranger handed money.*

TRANSFORMATIONS OF NUCLEAR SENTENCE A 3

Like nuclear sentence A 2, A 3 has all the transformations of nuclear sentence A 1. In fact the similarity is even greater, since only the O_2 may be placed at the left of the verb in the T-passive and the T-emphasis. The C must stay at the right of the verb.

The fact that the O_1 may be moved to the left of the verb and the C may not is of course a way of distinguishing between nuclear sentences A 2 and A 3.

• E X E R C I S E

Make five examples of each of the transformations regularly arising from the base nuclear sentences A 2 and A 3. Be sure you use at least one base sentence of the kind *The people forced him to run.*

TRANSFORMATIONS OF NUCLEAR SENTENCE B

In addition to the regular transformations for negative and question and the transformation for imperative, nuclear sentence B has two special transformations. One of these is signalled by an unstressed *there,* the other by *there* (stressed), *then* or some equivalent. These last two transformations are rather frequent in modern writing, especially with a few much-used verbs.

Negative transformation

The negative transformation is regular. Single-word verbs require the function word *do* with *not.* Multi-word verbs have the *not* between the first v and the rest of the verbs. Single-word verbs require *never* before the V; multi-word verbs may have the *never* either before or after the first v. Examples:

Children play. ~~⟫ Children do not play.
Children have been playing. ~~⟫ Children have not been playing.
Children play. ~~⟫ Children never play.
Children have played. ~~⟫ Children never have played.

or

Children have never played.

(Other negative transformations may be made by using the information under "Transformations of Nuclear Sentence A 1.")

Question transformation

Question transformations are also regular, *do* being required with all single-word verbs but *be,* and reversal of the first v and the S when a multi-word verb occurs. Examples:

Children play. ~~⟫ Do children play?
Children were playing ~~⟫ Were children playing?
The boy was here. ~~⟫ Was the boy here?

(Sentences with just $|^1S^1|$ $|^1V^1|$ are infrequent when the V is a single-word form of *be.* The M, *here,* is a modifier of *was,* not a C, since we would not write *The here boy was here.*)

Imperative transformation

The imperative transformation consists of the V_1 form of the verb, e.g.,

You go. ~~⟫ Go.
You write. ~~⟫ Write.

Unstressed-*there* transformation

The unstressed-*there* transformation is very frequent. In fact most of the B type nuclear sentences that have *be* for the verb appear in this transformation. It also is used with other verbs, especially *seem* and words that approximate the meanings of *be* and *seem,* such as *exist, happen, occur.* The verb *come* also is much used in this transformation. That the *there* that begins this transformation has lost its meaning as a direction-pointing word is illustrated by such a sentence as *There's plenty there,* in which the pointing feature has to be shown by an additional *there.* The unstressed *there* is, therefore, a mere grammatical signaller, having no meaning in the normal sense of the word. This is illustrated by the definitions given in dictionaries, such as this one from the *Century* dictionary: " *there* is often used as an indefinite grammatical subject in place of the real subject."

Examples: (Notice that the base sentences are unnatural. This is due of course to the fact that the transformation has in most discourse replaced the base sentence.)

> A tree is. ⟶ There is a tree.
> A dance will be. ⟶ There will be a dance.
> An accident has been. ⟶ There has been an accident.
> A time comes. ⟶ There comes a time.
> A reason seems. ⟶ There seems a reason.

This transformation also occurs with sentences that have modifiers, and these sentences furnish more natural base sentences.

> A tree is in the field. ⟶ There is a tree in the field.
> A large gathering was there. ⟶ There was a large gathering there.

Time-place transformation

Modifiers having to do with time and place may appear as sentence modifiers at the beginning of any nuclear sentence. But with certain verbs the appearance of the modifier in this position permits reversing the position of the S and the V. The whole verb, if it is a multi-word verb, may move to S position but often only the first v moves to S position. Just which verbs will allow this transformation has not been determined. *There* is often used as a modifier in beginning position. This makes for confusion between the T-time-place and the T-unstressed-*there*." This confusion will be avoided if you remember that *there* always has more than minimum stress in the T-time-place. Examples:

> My fiancé stood there. ⟶ There stood my fiancé.
> (Notice how differently the *there* is stressed than the beginning *there* in *There was an old man there*.)
> A parade came down the street. ⟶ Down the street came a parade.
> The climax had come hours before. ⟶ Hours before had come the climax.
>
> > *or*
>
> Hours before had the climax come.
> The courier rode through clouds of dust. ⟶ Through clouds of dust rode the courier.

(Preposition structures, single words or headword structures used as modifiers are most frequent in this transformation. Modifiers that are included nuclear sentences are very infrequently used.)

• EXERCISES

1. Make as many sentences as you can of the T-unstressed-*there* type without repeating the verb-shape. Use both single-word and multi-word verbs.
2. Do the same for T-time-place.
3. Use various types of modifiers to create time-place transformations. Try especially to create a sentence or two with included nuclear sentences as preceding sentence-modifiers, such as *When he left came the climax*.

TRANSFORMATIONS OF NUCLEAR SENTENCE C

The transformations for nuclear sentence C include, of course, T-negative, T-question, T-imperative, T-*it* and—rather infrequently—the T-emphasis. For the most part these transformations are similar to those described in connection with nuclear sentence A 1. But some differences exist; therefore each transformation will be discussed separately.

Negative transformation

The negative transformation uses the negative signallers *not* and *never* in much the same way as does nuclear sentence A 1. (Only the most frequent transformations are exemplified. For the others check the list under nuclear sentence A 1 and try the possibilities.)

> The men are vagrants. ⤳ The men are not vagrants.
> My son will be a freshman. ⤳ My son will not be a freshman.
> All trees are green. ⤳ All trees are not green.
> They have been happy. ⤳ They have not been happy.
> These men are candidates. ⤳ These men are never candidates.
> These men have been candidates. ⤳. These men have never been candidates.
>
> *or*
>
> These men never have been candidates.

But in addition to these regular transformations there is another, not so common, but certainly not strange appearing. This is illustrated by the sentence:

> He was my friend. ⤳ Never was he my friend.

We found a similar device among the transformations of nuclear sentence A 1, but it occurred only when the sentence had a multi-word V. With nuclear sentence C it occurs both with single-word V, as above, and with multi-word V, i.e.,

> He has been my friend. ⤳ Never has he been my friend.

The transformation with single-word V can happen only when the V is some form of *be*. *Become, seem* and the substitutes do not permit this transformation, as a few trial sentences will show.

Question transformation

The same conditions are apparent in this transformation as in the T-negative. Function words (*do, does, did*) are required with single-word verbs except when the V is a form of *be*. In the sentences with single-word *be* forms, a simple reversal of the S and the V creates a T-question. Examples:

My candidate became mayor. ⟶ Did my candidate become mayor?
Mother was very stern. ⟶ Was mother very stern?
I am lonesome. ⟶ Am I lonesome?
They are my associates. ⟶ Are they my associates?

When the verb is multi-word, the same conditions as in nuclear sentence A 1 are observed. The first v and the S reverse their positions.

We have become strangers. ⟶ Have we become strangers?
Those dogs will be sick. ⟶ Will those dogs be sick?

Imperative transformation

In this transformation also, the similarity to nuclear sentence A 1 is great. The base form must have an S that is *you* and a V that includes V_1. Since the V in nuclear sentence C is very often a column-2 form of *be* (*are*), the change from *are* to *be* must occur, and the shape with *You be* is possible. (See page 159.) Examples:

You become more studious. ⟶ Become more studious.
You are my hero. ⟶ Be my hero.

It transformation

As with nuclear sentence A 1 it is possible to postpone expressing the S until after the V and the C by starting the sentence with a meaningless *it*. This transformation occurs, as we have seen, much more frequently when S is something other than an N or a headword structure. Examples:

> When Chaucer was born is doubtful. ⟶ It is doubtful when Chaucer was born.
> To tease the animals is dangerous. ⟶ It is dangerous to tease the animals.
> Where to put all the books became a problem. ⟶ It became a problem where to put all the books.
> To work is no fun. ⟶ It's no fun to work.

In general the T-*it* seems closer to speech, thus less formal than the base forms from which it derives.

Emphasis transformation

This transformation puts the element following the V (in this structure a C) in front of the S. As we have said, this transformation is not very frequent in the dialect of most people, and is even more infrequent with nuclear sentence C than with A 1. Examples:

> John was an amateur. ⟶ An amateur John was.
> (This sounds quite abnormal and awkward.)
> She is a pretty girl. ⟶ A pretty girl she is.
> (This sounds more natural with an additional modifier, i.e.,
> She is a pretty girl but nothing more. ⟶
> A pretty girl she is but nothing more.)
> Father became suspicious. ⟶ Suspicious father became.
> (This, too, sounds pretty abnormal.)

Reverse transformation

Nuclear sentence C may often be reversed without particular awkwardness. This means that we may say either *The trees are tall* or *Tall are the trees*. But simple reversal does not always seem so possible. The sentence *The boys are hungry* does not seem quite acceptable as *Hungry are the boys*. Nor does the *The post office is a white building* seem quite comfortable as *A white building is the post office*. In fact there is not enough available information concerning the possibilities of reversing nuclear sentence C so that we can make any generalizations.

- E X E R C I S E S

1. Write ten nuclear sentences of the C type to serve as base sentences, and make all the possible transformations. If you can think of other transformations try them out. Your ten base sentences should include six with a form of *be* as the V, two with a form of *become* as the V and two with a form of *seem* as the V. You should have an equal number of single-word and multi-word V's. Write one example of each transformation in formula form.
2. From any five pages in a magazine collect all the C type sentences. See how many of them may acceptably be reversed. From your examination of the sentences can you make any tentative conclusion as to what kinds of C type nuclear sentences can be reversed and what not?

The discussion of nuclear sentence transformations just concluded does not exhaust the subject. It must be emphasized that these are the commonest and most frequently used transformations. It must also be reiterated that the transformations may be transformed. For example a negative transformation may undergo a question transformation, e.g.,

> Little girls do not like rough games. ➤
> Do not (don't) little girls like rough games?

Or an unstressed-*there* transformation may undergo a question transformation, e.g.,

> There had been an accident. ➤ Had there been an accident?

which in turn may undergo a negative transformation:

> Had not (hadn't) there been an accident?

In addition to these normal developments, unusual transformations of nuclear sentences in order to get special emphasis or to attract attention are made by writers. Such a reversal of type A 1 as *He planned teaching* ⤳ *Teaching planned he* is not impossible, largely because there is no likelihood of thinking that the O_2 is *he*. Or a type C such as *Mary seemed happy then* ⤳ *Then seemed Mary happy* may occur.

Writers of English are always experimenting with new ways of transforming the nuclear sentences, sometimes successfully, often not. Poets in particular get restless within the bounds of normal English and attempt to break through the barriers. Poets of course are especially aware of the barriers of normal English because so often the rhythm singing in their brains will not adjust itself to the requirements of normal English syntax structures.

• EXERCISES

1. Take three different regular transformations of a nuclear sentence and see how many additional transformations can be made from them.
2. Try to create some transformations both from the five nuclear sentence types and from transformations of the base sentences that you are not aware of having seen before. Do you think they are intelligible?
3. What are the base structures from which the following transformations are made? Write the base structure, using all the part-of-speech words in the sentences, and label it. Also name the transformation (or transformations) involved. Some of the transformations may not be normal ones. Write the formula for each base structure.

    a. Half serpent in the struggle grow these worms.
    b. I the death of Love had deeply planned.
    c. Why did I come here in that dullard fit?
    d. Such play as this the devils might appall.
    e. What a dusty answer gets the soul.
    f. Tired of his dark dominion swung the fiend
       above the rolling ball.

g. Around the ancient track marched, rank on rank,
   the army of unalterable law.

h. Mindful were the ploughmen.

i. Slack the thistle-head piled its down-silk grey.

j. Pleasant ran our thinking.

k. Never in woods runs white instantly fleeing itself.

l. Death his people had dealt their dam and their sire.

m. It seemed that drafts he had drunk of clear Hippocrene.

n. Him Phoebus many lessons and counsels gave.

o. Sick or maimed or them that, frenzied in some delirious
   rage, outran the measure, his juice of the woods reclaimed.

(These sentences are taken from or adapted from the poems of George Meredith entitled "Modern Love," "Lucifer in Starlight," "Phoebus with Admetus" and "Melampus.")

TRANSFORMATIONS OF NUCLEAR SENTENCES INVOLVING INTERROGATORS

The list of interrogators is short:

who (whom, whose)

which	where
what	why
when	how

As we saw in Chapter VI the function of these words when they appear at the beginning of a sentence is to signal that a question is coming, unless some other signal denies this later on in the sentence. In such a sentence as *Which of the two boys was the guilty one was difficult to decide,* the question signal is denied when we recognize that the apparent nuclear sentence underlined at the beginning is an S and therefore an included nuclear sentence. Until this happens, however, everything points to a T-question.

The transformations involving pure interrogators are relatively simple. The words involved are *when, where, why* and *how.*

Question transformation

Using type A 1 as the base:

The gentleman wants his lunch. ⟶ When does the gentleman want his lunch?

Notice: The single-word verb must change to a multi-word verb with the appropriate form of *do* as an auxiliary, and the added auxiliary moves to the left of the S.

The girl will announce her engagement. ⟶ When will the girl announce her engagement?
(When the base has a multi-word verb the first auxiliary moves to the left of the subject.)

Using types A 2 and A 3 as the base:

He gave them the apples. ⟶ When did he give them the apples?
He will write them his decision. ⟶ When will he write them his decision?
They chose him their favorite student. ⟶ When did they choose him their favorite student?
We will find him dull. ⟶ When will we find him dull?

Using nuclear sentence B as the base:

Children play in the yard. ⟶ When do children play in the yard?
He had been planning. ⟶ When had he been planning?
(The transformation is like that for types A 1 and C.)

Using nuclear sentence C as the base:

That gentleman was ready ⟶ When was that gentleman ready?
(The single-word verb *was* moves to the left of the subject.)

That young man will be available. ⟶ When will that young man be available?
(This T-question is formed like the transformation of the multi-word verb variant of type A 1.)

That man became the owner. ⟶ When did that man become the owner?

Notice: Only single-word *be* forms can be moved to the left of S. All other single-word verbs must add an auxiliary (*do*). The general rule for T-question with interrogator *when* is: Place *when* at the beginning of the sentence and place a single form of *be* or the first auxiliary of a multi-word verb at the left of the subject. If a single-word verb other than *be* is involved, the appropriate form of *do* must be added at the left of the subject and the V must become V_1.

Testing with *where, why* and *how* will show that the rule just stated will apply with them just as with *when*. The essential feature is that the lexical verb, if a single-word form of *be*, should move to the left of the subject or, for any other verb, an auxiliary—added if necessary—should be at the left of the subject. This is essentially the same procedure as in making the T-question without an interrogator. The rule thus may be stated: Perform the normal T-question and prefix the interrogator.

The transformations using the functional interrogators *who, which* and *what* present more complications. *Who,* especially, because of its inflected forms, is rather difficult to deal with. It must be emphasized that the use of the inflected forms of *who* differs in writing from what it is in speech. Almost any speaker is likely to say in colloquial language *Who's he writing to?* i.e., /huz hi raytən tu/, but a similar structure in written English would more probably appear as *Whom is he writing to?* or *To whom is he writing?* The statements below all refer to written English.

We must also recognize that the base sentence must be conceived as having a word different from the functional interrogator, whether it be *who, which* or *what*. For example, the base from which *Who wrote the letter?* is made must be thought of as *Someone wrote the letter.* In other words the insertion of the int$_N$ in place of one word in the base is part of the transformation.

Question transformation with *who, (whom, whose)* as interrogator

The form *who* appears in the subject position in writing.

Someone broke the window. ⟶ Who broke the window?
Someone is John. ⟶ Who is John?
Someone is arriving. ⟶ Who is arriving?

Someone gave you the message. ⟶ Who gave you the message?
Someone made him happy. ⟶ Who made him happy?

In this transformation only the substitution of *who* for the subject of the base is required.

The form *whom* appears in O_2 or O_1 position or as N_{pr} in writing. It cannot be used in a T based on nuclear sentences B or C.

He hit somebody. ⟶ Whom did he hit?

The O_2 becomes the first word in the sentence. The single-word verb, as is true in most T-questions, must have an auxiliary *do* provided. This follows the *whom* and precedes the S.

If the verb has one or more auxiliaries the first auxiliary follows the O_2 and precedes the S.

His conduct has displeased someone. ⟶ Whom has his conduct displeased?
The nurse was giving the woman someone. ⟶ Whom was the nurse giving the woman?

or

The nurse was giving someone the child. ⟶ Whom was the nurse giving the child?

The first of the two A 2 sentences above would not appear frequently, since the occasions for having an O_2 that can be replaced by *whom* in this structure are rather infrequent. In the second the *whom* would more frequently be an N_{pr} with the preposition *to* either just before it or at the very end of the sentence, i.e., *To whom was the nurse giving the child?* or *Whom was the nurse giving the child to?*

They will elect someone class representative. ⟶ Whom will they elect class representative?

In type A 3 no complications arise.

The form *whom* as N_{pr} has been mentioned just above. It seems that a choice is almost always available as to whether the pr should immediately precede *whom* or appear as the last word in the sentence. The following sentences illustrate the use of *whom* as N_{pr} in nuclear sentences A 1, B and C.

> You bought that book for someone. ⟶ Whom did you buy that book for? *or* For whom did you buy that book?
> He was becoming very angry with someone. ⟶ With whom was he becoming angry? *or* Whom was he becoming angry with?
> They will worry about someone. ⟶ Whom will they worry about? *or* About whom will they worry?

The A 2 and the A 3 types do not present any new complications. It is quite impossible to predict where the preposition best goes. The first two of the three sentences above seem to me better with the preposition in front of *whom*. The third seems better with the preposition at the end.

The form *whose* appears as S, O_2, O_1, C, N_{pr} and also as a modifier of all these. The use of *whose* as O_1 is rather rare and so is its use as the C in an A 3 nuclear sentence. The transformations follow the practices for *who* and *whom*. Examples of each use are given below with no further comment.

> S   Somebody's hit the target. ⟶ Whose hit the target?
> O_2 I broke somebody's. ⟶ Whose did I break?
> C   This is somebody's. ⟶ Whose is this.
> O_1 I gave somebody's a push. ⟶ Whose did I give a push?
> C   You made me somebody's. ⟶ Whose did you make me?
> N_{pr} The cat has pounced on somebody's. ⟶ Whose has the cat pounced on? *or* On whose has the cat pounced?
> C   Somebody's lunch is lost. ⟶ Whose lunch is lost?

Question transformation with *which* and *what* as interrogators

Since *which* and *what* have no inflectional forms, no problem of selection among forms arises. *Which* and *what* when used as interrogators require exactly similar operations to *who*. They may appear as S, O_2, O_1, C, N_{pr} and as a modifier of any of these. Examples can be easily worked out on the model of *who, whom, whose*. The words *a selection* can be used in the base sentence to represent *which* and the word *something* to represent *what*.

A final note

When writing formulas it is necessary to treat pr int$_{N_{pr}}$ as a sentence modifier, as below.

You had planned the surprise for someone
For whom had you planned the surprise?
[^{1}pr int$_{N_{pr}}^1$] |^{1}v$_4^1$| |^{1}N$_p^1$| |^{1}V$_5^1$| |^{1}O$_2^1$| ?

Whom had you planned the surprise for?
[^{1}int$_{N_{pr}}^1$] |^{1}v$_4^1$| |^{1}N$_p^1$| |^{1}V$_5^1$| |^{1}O$_2^1$| [^{1}pr^1] ?

• E X E R C I S E S

1. Write twenty sentences and transform them into questions using the pure interrogators that are appropriate.
2. Write twenty sentences, using among the sentences all the functional interrogators. Then write the base sentences from which these may be derived.
3. Write the formulas for each of the base sentences made above and for the question sentences that you developed from them.

TRANSFORMATIONS OF INCLUDED NUCLEAR SENTENCES

The transformations of included nuclear sentences that use pure includers are for the most part like the transformations of non-included nuclear sentences. The includer is simply added at the beginning of the transformation. However, T-question and T-imperative cannot appear. The T-reverse of Type C and the T-emphasis of types A 1, A 2 and A 3 are more unusual in included nuclear sentences than in non-included nuclear sentences. Some examples follow; others should be worked out, using the list of includers in Chapter VI.

T-passive	when he finished the work ⟶ when the work was finished by him (or without *by him*)
T-negative	when he was busy ⟶ when he was not busy because he hesitated ⟶ because he never hesitated since he had won ⟶ since he never had won *or* since he had never won *or* since never had he won
T-reverse	though the lea was lovely ⟶ though lovely was the lea
T-emphasis	inasmuch as he sought prestige only ⟶ inasmuch as prestige only he sought
T-unstressed-*there*	before a single person was there ⟶ before there was a single person there
T-time-place	while a policeman stood by the automobile ⟶ while by the automobile stood a policeman
T-*it*	providing to keep in touch was possible ⟶ providing it was possible to keep in touch

The includer *if* has an alternate structure involving a change in the position of the verb. It also involves the use of the subjunctive forms of the verb when they are appropriate. The subjunctive forms are V_1 for all verbs except *be*; for this verb, the subjunctive forms are *be* and *were*. These are not new or additional forms to those in the verb paradigm, but they are distributed differently from their usual distributions. The V_1 form and the *be* form are used with *he, she, it* and singular nouns. The *be* is also used with *I*. The *were* form is used with *I* and with *he, she, it* and singular nouns. Generally the forms appear in included nuclear sentences which have *if* as the includer. (See Chapter VI.) Examples:

> If he be successful, it will be a surprise.
> If I be reproached, I will resign.
> If he were here, he would defend me.

But also we may have the equivalent meaning by reversing the auxiliary and the subject. Not all structures seem natural in this form. *Be he successful it will be a surprise* sounds at least very old fashioned, but *Were he here, he would defend me* sounds quite usual.

Verb forms other than the subjunctive forms also appear. For example:

Had he the height, he'd be a great basketball player.
Had he been approached, he would have accepted.

• EXERCISE

Try the subjunctive form described immediately above with several single and multi-word verbs and work out statements about your own usage.

The transformations of included nuclear sentences using functional includers are similar to the question transformations that use functional interrogators, as would be expected, since three of the four functional includers most frequently used are also shapes that are included in the list of functional interrogators. That is, we cannot simply prefix the includer to a normal transformation of a non-included nuclear sentence. This is because the includer becomes an element in the included nuclear sentence. We must therefore use as the base for the transformations a non-included nuclear sentence.

As with the interrogators it is necessary to deal separately with the three forms of *who,* which are distributed differently in writing.

Transformations with *who*

who as C: John is somebody ⟶ who John is

The form is identical with the T-question, of course, except that it doesn't begin with a capital letter and doesn't necessarily have a mark of punctuation after it.

who as C: John is somebody ⟶ who John is

Notice: This transformation is different from the T-question because the C is followed by the S, not by either a V or a v.

whom as O_2:   He attacked someone ⟿ whom he attacked

Notice: The O_2 is followed by the S, not by the v or V as in a question.

whom as O_1:   He issued someone the pass ⟿ whom he issued the pass

Again notice that the O_1 simply moves to beginning of the structure leaving the rest unchanged. Of course this structure would be more likely to appear as *whom he issued the pass to.*

whom as N_{pr}:   He asked about somebody ⟿ about whom he asked
　　　　　　　　　or whom he asked about

Here we have the choice of putting the preposition just before the N_{pr} when it moves to the beginning of the structure or at the very end of the structure.

　　　　whose as S: Somebody's was there ⟿ whose was there

This would appear as an S in such a sentence as *Whose was there was uncertain* or as O_2 in *We didn't know whose was there.*

whose as C: It is somebody's ⟿ whose it is
whose as O_1:   We gave somebody's the preference ⟿ whose we gave the preference
This would be more usual as *whose we gave the preference to.*

whose as N_{pr}:   He inquired for somebody's ⟿ for whose he inquired
　　　　　　　　　or whose he inquired for
　whose as M: Someone's part was important ⟿ whose part was important
　　　　　　　　　We found it in someone's purse ⟿ in whose purse we found it

Transformations with *which*

Which may be used in all the ways in which *who, whom, whose* are used, that is as S, O_2, O_1, C, N_{pr} and M.

Which as S: The horse ran well ⟶ which ran well
 as O_2:   He owned a horse ⟶ which he owned
 as O_1:   He gave the horse plenty of hay ⟶ which he gave plenty of hay
 as C: The betting made his horse the favorite ⟶ which the betting made his horse
 as N_{pr}:   He refused many offers for the horse ⟶ for which he refused many offers *or* which he refused many offers for
 as M: He ran that race well ⟶ which race he ran well

This last usage is not highly favored by expert writers, but it occurs now and then.

Transformations with *what*

You will of course have recognized that the included nuclear sentences described above may be either modifiers or noun-substitutes. The *what* transformations are only noun-substitutes.

What as S: Something came next ⟶ what came next
 as O_2:   He wanted something ⟶ what he wanted
 as O_1:   He would give something his attention ⟶ what he would give his attention

As with the other functional includers, this seems more natural with a *to* at the end.

 as C: The decision was something ⟶ what the decision was
as N_{pr}:   He was working with something ⟶ what he was working with

This regularly appears in this form rather than with the pr in front of the *what*. This, of course, is caused by the N-quality of the included nuclear sentence with *what,* which often makes the structure itself an N_{pr}. The sentence *He was dissatisfied with what he was working with* illustrates the point. The pr before *what* has for N_{pr} the whole structure. The pr at the end has *what* for its N_{pr}. The formula for this structure is:

$$(^1pr \; \underline{[i_{N_{pr}}] \; |^1N_p{}^1| \; |^1v_4V_3{}^1| \; [pr]}^1)$$

or in general terms $(^1pr \; N_{pr}{}^1)$.

The two pr's can be distinguished by noticing whether any doubtful example can occur at the end. If it can, then its N_{pr} is *what;* if it can't, then its N_{pr} is the whole included nuclear sentence. But there will be few questionable examples, since it is regular practice to distinguish the functions of each pr by its position.

Transformations with *that*

The transformations with the includer *that* may be either noun-substitutes or modifiers. But since the shape *that* is regularly used as a noun modifier, as in *that man, that plan, that can,* it cannot appear as i_{NM}. *That* is used regularly as an alternate to *who* and *whom* in sentences that do not have a single-bar juncture before the beginning of the included nuclear sentence. This practice avoids the necessity of choosing between *who* and *whom.*

that as S:	Something came easily ⤳ that came easily	
	Someone loves you ⤳ that loves you	
as O_2:	John wanted something ⤳ that John wanted	
as O_1:	I gave something some attention ⤳ that I gave some attention	
	(It would seem quite as natural to say *that I gave some attention to.*)	
as C:	Mary was something ⤳ that Mary was	
as N_{pr}:	James was president of something ⤳ that James was president of	

Notice: The pr with *that* always comes at the end of the structure. Any pr at the beginning has for its N_{pr} the *whole following structure*

• EXERCISE

Write sentences that will illustrate all of the included nuclear sentences described above.

TRANSFORMATIONS OF THE REMAINING SYNTAX STRUCTURES

The four remaining syntax structures have far fewer transformations than do the nuclear sentences and the included nuclear sentences. This probably is due to the unconscious realization by speakers of the language that the nuclear sentences are fundamental units of discourse and that any attempts to get special effects and thus more satisfactory responses should be made in these structures. In any event, the other structures have a rigidity of structure that is not often tampered with.

We should remember that any unit of discourse can express a question by the use of a double-bar juncture in speech or a question mark in writing. Rather infrequently in writing, one of these structures will appear followed by a question mark. This practice is most frequent in rather informal writing.

Transformations of predicate structures

Since predicate structures in writing are almost composed of the forms V_1 (often with *to*) or V_3 plus O_2, O_1 or C in appropriate combinations, the chances of variation in word order are few. Shifting a following O_1 or O_2 before the V would invariably make it subject, especially since the subject and the O_2 and O_1 have the same shape when they are pronouns in this particular sort of included predication structure.

However, predicate structures may have negative transformations:

We planned *to buy them.* ➤ We planned *not to buy them.*

Placing the *not* between *to* and *buy* is frequent, though frowned on as a split infinitive by some people. Placing the *not* after *them* is also possible but may be considered "poetic."

> He wrote about *studying his lessons.* ⟶
> He wrote about *not studying his lessons.*

The *not* is pretty well fixed in this version, except for the unusual but possible placement after the O_2.

The predicate structures based on nuclear sentences A 1, A 2 and A 3 may also be transformed for passive.

> He talked about *planting a tree.* ⟶ He talked about *a tree being planted.*
> He resolved on *reading them a lecture.* ⟶ He resolved on *them being read a lecture.* or He resolved on *a lecture being read them.*
> The meeting finally ended by appointing him treasurer. ⟶ The meeting finally ended by *him being appointed treasurer.*

Many writers would think that this last T should be written *his being appointed treasurer.* However it seems more consistent to think of *being appointed treasurer* as modified by *his* and consequently as a substitute for an N, the whole structure (*his being appointed treasurer*) being the N_{pr} after *by. His being appointed treasurer* therefore would not be a transformation. This approach makes it unnecessary to introduce a new factor in the T-passive of this type.

> We wanted *to please him.* ⟶ We wanted *him to be pleased.*

The predicate structure with V_1 and based on types A 1 and A 3 only awkwardly make T-passive and may be disregarded.

It is noticeable that the T-passive of these predicate structures tend to be understood in a much more general sense than do the base forms. *We wanted to please him,* for example, identifies the potential "pleasers," but *We wanted him to be pleased* does not. This generalizing effect seems a regular feature of the T-passive and, of course, may be the reason for its existence.

Other transformations of predicate structures do not seem possible.

• EXERCISE

Work out transformations for all the types of predicate structures. Can you find any that you think are workable?

Transformations of headword structures

Both included nuclear sentences and predicate structures are close in structural features to nuclear sentences. In a very real sense they are transformations of nuclear sentences, though it is convenient to keep the three in separate classes. Headword structures, however, do not resemble nuclear sentences. They consist of a single headword, plus what we can call reduced nuclear sentences, all tending to make more precise and exact—more denotative—the total meaning of the structure. Thus almost the only possible transformations must involve changes of position of the modifiers in relation to the headword. This topic has already been discussed briefly in Chapter VII.

In general, single-word modifiers of nouns come before the noun and inside the marker (if there is a marker) and multi-word modifiers follow the noun. (There are exceptions, of course, but not many. For instance *both* always comes outside the marker and *alone* always comes after the noun, presumably to distinguish it from *a lone* in speech.) But by use of single-bar juncture, often but not always marked by a comma, this normal practice can be modified, and a transformation may result. The effect of such a transformation is generally to draw attention to the modifier in the abnormal position. This transformation may be called T-emphasis.

> *A solitary old man* stood by the grave. ⟶
> *An old man, solitary,* stood by the grave.

This is perhaps a more common practice with V_3 and V_5 modifiers.

> *The dejected little boy* trudged dolefully away. ⟶
> *The little boy, dejected,* trudged dolefully away.

The exulting girl accepted the diamond. ⟶
The girl, exulting, accepted the diamond.

The essential feature other than position is of course the use of the single-bar juncture. This feature may also be used with single-word adjectives outside the marker to get pretty much the same effect.

Solitary, an old man stood beside the grave.
Dejected, the little boy trudged dolefully away.
Exulting, the girl accepted the diamond.

The same emphasis on the modifier may be attained with modifiers that are coordination structures by placing them either after the headword or outside the marker and using a single-bar juncture to mark them. Examples:

The startled or confused man seemed unable to reply. ⟶
The man, startled or confused, seemed unable to reply.
or
Startled or confused, the man seemed unable to reply.
The stark, bare tree stood out against the sunset. ⟶
The tree, stark and bare, stood out against the sunset.

Though many writers do not always or even regularly supply a comma in these transformations, it is impossible to read the sentence aloud slowly without the juncture being audible.

Multi-word modifiers that are neither included nuclear sentences nor preposition structures may move to the left of the headword and outside the marker (if a marker occurs). Only those multi-word modifiers accompanied by single-bar junctures in normal position can move thus.

The boxer, tough as nails, moved in for the kill. ⟶
Tough as nails, the boxer moved in for the kill.
The team, elated by its victory, tore down the posters. ⟶
Elated by its victory, the team tore down the posters.
Smith, blasted by the critics, withdrew his play. ⟶

Blasted by the critics, Smith withdrew his play.

The various changes of position all seem to be made to draw attention to the unit changed from its normal position and thus to emphasize it.

Transformations of preposition structures

The only transformation of preposition structures that seems possible is the one discussed previously that involves included nuclear sentences with functional includers. This transformation enables the preposition to appear at the end of the structure when its N_{pr} is a functional includer. The transformation occurs with all functional includers and with no other N_{pr}.

Transformations of coordination structures

These transformations involve only the presence or absence of coordinators and have been discussed both in Chapter VII and above in the section on transformations of headword structures. The transformation rule may be stated as: Coordinators may be omitted and marked by a comma or, when nuclear sentences are the units being coordinated, by a semicolon.

• EXERCISE

Try all kinds of modifiers in changed positions, including preposition structures and included nuclear sentences. See if you can find others not mentioned here.

Notes

CHAPTER I

1. "Time-binding" means holding past, present and future together. Human beings are the only creatures who, learning about the past, are able to use this learning to talk about the future. An example: "Now that we have found out how to hit the ball, we should have better success tomorrow."

2. "Neural events" are those events occurring inside the body, often as a result of something in the outside world, that impel a person to make the sounds of speech.

3. Writing cannot preserve the sounds of people's voices and thus it cannot reveal the individual's vocal habits, which so often improve (or make less effective) communication. Also writing cannot give us the appearance of the individual—his gestures and facial expressions. Nowadays, however, we can combine picture with sound on film to preserve not only the sound but also the appearance of the speaker. One sometimes wonders if these technical improvements mean the diminishing importance of writing.

4. In the twentieth century, too, scholars become upset when something familiar is changed. See the reviews of *Webster's Third New International* in *Dictionaries and That Dictionary* edited by James Sledd and Wilma R. Ebbitt (Chicago; Scott, Foresman & Co., 1962). A recent British translation of the Bible has stimulated similar violent protests. See especially T. S. Eliot's article in the London *Observer,* reprinted in *The National Observer,* December 24, 1962.

5. The preceding remarks—it is perhaps unnecessary to remind the reader—pertain to language as defined on page 4. They do not pertain

to writing, which does have clear standards that prevail over the entire English-speaking territory and are respected by skilled writers as regularly in Scotland and Australia as in Iowa.

CHAPTER II

1. The levels are called primary ('), secondary (ˆ), tertiary (`) and minimum (x). The last is seldom marked. In talking about stress it is customary to call syllables spoken at the lowest level (x) "unstressed." When we speak of a "stressed" syllable we mean, therefore, a syllable with one of the upper three levels of stress (' ˆ `).

2. All written symbols for single phonemes and all material written with symbols for phonemes are identified by being enclosed in slant lines.

3. A morpheme is the smallest unit of meaning in a language. For example, *un-* in *uninteresting,* which means *not,* is a morpheme. See Chapter III.

CHAPTER III

1. When two or more units, whether they are allomorphs or allophones, cannot be substituted freely for one another they are said to be in "complementary distribution." Thus in making nouns plural we have only one choice among /s/, /z/ or /z/ for any particular word. We do not say /rowds/ even though it is pronounceable; we must say /rowdz/.

2. The base form of a word, a morpheme or a structure is the one arbitrarily selected by grammarians to start from in deriving other forms. We say *dog* is the base form and that we make the plural by adding *s*. It would be exactly the same if we said *dogs* was the base form and we made the singular by dropping the *s*. The choice of a base form is, thus, completely arbitrary. In general the form that appears at the beginning of a principal entry in a dictionary is used as the base form of a word.

CHAPTER IV

1. These six answers illustrate the nuclear sentence and the five word-groups described in this chapter and in Chapter VII. The name

for these five word-groups is "syntax structure," and each one has a name of its own, one or two of which are quite familiar, e.g., the second one, which is a "prepositional phrase."

2. A discourse is a total speech or writing unit marked off by some inescapable beginning and ending.

3. These three punctuation marks, you remember, are the written symbols of the end-of-sentence junctures.

4. A list and description of the uses of all the symbols in this book will be found in Appendix I.

5. In the system of symbols used in this book a vertical line marks the beginning and the end of each part of the nuclear sentence.

6. The reason for the O_2 will be explained later. O_2 may be called "direct" object if you wish.

7. O_1 may be called "indirect" object if you wish.

8. C may be called "complement" if you wish. O_2, of course, is "direct object."

CHAPTER V

1. A word might be said here about proper and common nouns. This distinction probably wouldn't have to be made except for writing. Consequently we should define the distinction only in terms of writing. Proper nouns we will define as those nouns that customarily begin with a capital letter even when they are not at the beginning of a sentence. They have to be learned, since no speech equivalent for a capital letter in such positions exists.

2. These words are inflected like *who*, i.e., *whomever, whomsoever.*

3. The plain form may be defined as the form listed in a dictionary at the beginning of the entry.

4. The forms in brackets show the previously listed forms that are used in the same distribution as the other forms in the column. The form *let* is used like the form *sung*, for example.

I have let the house. I have sung the song.

5. The bulk of English verbs, all but about a hundred in fact, are in the 4-form group.

6. The forms *am, are* and *be* do not belong theoretically with *is,*

since they are not alternate forms, but this is a convenient place to list them. The forms *was* and *were* are, of course, singular and plural respectively, not alternates. No other verb makes this distinction in Modern English. *Be* is further complicated by the use in the subjunctive of the form *be* with all nouns and pronouns and *were* with *I* and *he*. The subjunctive will be discussed later.

7. The names are "infinitive" for Column I, "third person singular, present tense" for Column 2, "present participle" or "gerund" (depending on distribution) for Column 3, "past tense" for Column 4, "past participle" for Column 5.

8. Modification is also performed by structures. In a following chapter the use of various syntax structures as modifiers will be discussed.

9. But what is said applies to all the syntax structures to be described in Chapter VI as well as to the nuclear sentences.

10. There are, as usual, exceptions to this generalization. The word *alone* always follows the noun it modifies, *Man alone among all the creatures on earth has a language.* The word *only* appears outside the marker as well as after the noun modified and of course in the normal position.

> Only the men can enter.
> The men only can enter.
> The only men available were the husbands of the officers.

The meaning that *only* adds to the sentence in the third example is different from that it adds in the first two. This fact no doubt accounts for the variety of positions occupied by *only*. There are a number of other exceptions: *only* and *alone* are merely samples.

In the third example above there is an example of a modifier other than *alone* and *only* coming after the noun modified. This is the word *available*. This usage is quite common, and many examples can be thought of, such as, *The only way possible to take* or *a great deal of money ready*. In all these examples, though, the modifier may be placed between the marker and the noun without damage to the meaning of the sentence.

11. Of course if there are two or more modifiers to the same word

one must come before the other. In *the big brick house,* both *big* and *brick* modify house. In the sentence *Children play here in the park,* both *here* and *in the park* modify play.

12. "Complementary distribution" is defined in note 1 of Chapter III (p. 192).

CHAPTER VI

1. If it were not so awkward, perhaps the term "part-of-speech in-cluder" would be a better name, since the functional includers serve as noun- or modifier-substitutes.

2. The words *can* and *will* are sometimes lexical verbs (V) but with a very special meaning.

3. In speech and occasionally in writing, *get* is used with a V_3 form to mean "start." *He got going. Will they ever get moving?*

4. Most speakers and writers would probably express this idea by *She will arrive before we get there.*

A List of Symbols and Formulas

A. Parts of Speech

Noun (N) and *Pronoun* (N$_p$)

Functions: S First element in nuclear sentences A, B, C.

O$_1$ First post-V element in nuclear sentence A 2.

O$_2$ Post-V element in nuclear sentence A 1; second post-V element in nuclear sentence A 2; first post-V element in nuclear sentence A 3.

C Second post-V element in nuclear sentence A 3; post-V element in nuclear sentence C.

N$_{pr}$ (or N$_{p/pr}$) A noun (or a noun substitute) following a preposition that attaches the noun to the sentence.

Verb (V)

Verbs are identified by the number of the columns in the following paradigm.

	1 (V$_1$)	2 (V$_2$)	3 (V$_3$)	4 (V$_4$)	5 (V$_5$)
3-form verbs	let	lets	letting	let	let
4-form verbs	place	places	placing	placed	placed
5-form verbs	sing	sings	singing	sang	sung
8-form verbs	be	(am	being	(was	been
		is		were)	
		are			
		be)			

V is the unclassified single-word verb or multi-word verb plus its modifiers in a generalized structure formula.

Modifier (M)

> *Adjectives* (M_A) — Must have a contrasting form in *–ly* that is distributed complementarily.
>
> *Adverbs* (M_{AV}) — Forms in *–ly* that have a contrasting form without *–ly*, which is distributed complementarily to M_A.
>
> (M_N) — Modifiers that are normally classified as nouns.
>
> M_{V_1}, M_{V_3}, M_{V_5} — Modifiers that are normally classified as verbs.
>
> Mp — Modifiers that are pronouns. This class includes genitives of pronouns, all numbers and such words as *some, any, that, such, this, few, many.*

B. Function Words

Noun Markers (m) — The markers are: *a, an, the, my, our, your, their.*

Prepositions (pr) — See the list in Chapter VI.

Auxiliary verbs (v) — Combine with V_1, V_3, V_5 verbs to form multi-word verbs.

> Two types
>
> Pure auxiliaries — See the list in Chapter VI.
>
> Auxiliaries that can be lexical ("meaning") verbs. See the list in Chapter VI.

Coordinators (c) — The coordinators are: *and, but, or, nor, for,* plus the correlatives *both . . . and, not only . . . but, either . . . or, neither . . . nor.*

Includers (i) —

> Two types
>
> Pure includers (i) — See the list in Chapter VI.
>
> Functional includers (i_N) or (i_M) — See the list in Chapter VI.

Interrogators (int) — See the list in Chapter VI.

> Two types
>
> > Pure interrogators — (int)
> >
> > Functional interrogators — (int_N) or (int_M)

C. The General Formulas for the Six Syntax Structures

1. Nuclear Sentences

Nuclear sentence A 1:   Authors write books.

$$|S| \qquad |V| \qquad |O_2|$$

Nuclear sentence A 2:   They gave him a medal.

$$|S| \quad |V| \quad |O_1| \qquad |O_2|$$

Nuclear sentence A 3:   Spring makes the grass green.

$$|S| \qquad |V| \qquad\quad |O_2| \quad |C|$$

Nuclear sentence B: Dogs bark.

$$|S| \quad |V|$$

Nuclear sentence C: Boys become men.

$$|S| \qquad |V| \quad |C|$$

The elements of nuclear sentences have their boundaries marked by numbered vertical lines. The superscripts enable the boundaries of two or more nuclear sentences (included or not included) in the same sentence to be distinguished.

He wrote, after he had overstayed his welcome, an insolent letter to the hostess.

$$|^1N_p{}^1| \quad |^1V_4 \leftarrow (^1i|^2N_p{}^2| \quad |^2{}_{V_4}V_5{}^2| \quad |^2M\ N^2|^1),\ ^1| \quad |^1m\ M_A\ N^1| \quad [^1\text{pr}\ \underline{m\ N}_{pr}{}^1].$$

2. The Headword Structure

M N is the simplest form with a noun headword. However there may be several M's, one of which is often an m. There may be structure-modifiers that follow, such as preposition structures or included nuclear sentences. When structures modify a particular word, parentheses enclose the structure and an arrow points to the word modified.

Examples: people on the beach

$$N \leftarrow (^1\text{pr}\ m\ N_{pr}{}^1)$$

people who like swimming

$$N \leftarrow (^1|^1i_N{}^1| \quad |^1V_1{}^1| \quad |^1N^1|^1)$$

V M or M V are the simplest formulas when the headword is a V, but as is true about N headwords, there may be one or more structures or additional single-word modifiers attached. The same use of ( ) is prescribed. M M is the simplest formula when an M is the headword, but the headword also may have several modifiers, either single words or structures.

3. *The Preposition Structure*

pr N_{pr} is the simplest form. The N_{pr} may be and frequently is some other structure, such as a headword structure. If N_{pr} is a structure a line should be drawn under the structure and pr added at the right end of the line.

Examples: in the brown coat

    pr $\underline{\text{m M}}$ N_{pr}

for what he could get

    pr $\underline{\left|^{1}i_{N}^{1}\right| \quad \left|^{1}N^{1}\right| \quad \left|^{1}v_{1} V_{1}^{1}\right|}_{pr}$

(This structure is a "transformation.")

Often, included nuclear sentences end with a pr whose N_{pr} (always a functional includer) is at the beginning of the structure. This situation may be dealt with as in the following example.

    They knew whom he was waiting for.

    $\left|^{1}Np^{1}\right| \quad \left|^{1}V_{4}^{1}\right| \quad \left|^{1} [N_{pr}] \quad \right|^{2}N_{p}^{2}\right| \quad \left|^{2}v_{4} \ V_{3}^{2}\right| \quad [pr] \ ^{1}|.$

The first broken line says that the structure is not complete but will continue later on. The second broken line marks the beginning of the continuation of the structure which is, as usual, ended with a solid bracket.

    They saw which class he had prepared for.

    $\left|^{1}N_{p}^{1}\right| \quad \left|^{1}V_{4}^{1}\right| \quad \left|^{1} [i_{M} N_{pr}] \quad \right|^{1}N_{p}^{1}\right| \quad \left|^{1}v_{4} \ V_{5}^{1}\right| \quad [pr] \ ^{1}|.$

4. *The Included Nuclear Sentence*

The formula is that of the nuclear sentence (or its transformation) plus or containing the word called an "includer." Pure includers are prefixed to the predication structures that are to be included. Functional includers are either prefixed or form part of a preposition structure that serves as a group includer.

Examples:

Pure Includer   He waited *while I wrote the letter.*

    $\left|^{1}N_{p}^{1}\right| \quad \left|^{1}V_{4}\right| \ \leftarrow \ (^{1}i|^{2}N_{p}^{2}| \quad |^{2}V_{4}^{2}|, \quad |^{2}mN^{2}|^{1}) \ |.$

Functional Includer   That is the dog *which howled all night.*

    $\left|^{1}N_{p}^{1}\right| \quad \left|^{1}V_{2}^{1}\right| \quad |^{1}m \ N \ \leftarrow \ (^{1}|^{2}i_{N} \ V_{4} \ \leftarrow \ (^{2}M \ N^{2}) \ ^{1})^{2}|^{1}|.$

Group Functional Includer   This is the diploma *for which I worked.*

$|^1N_p{}^1|$ $|^1V_2{}^1|$ $|^1m\ N$ $\leftarrow$ $(^1[^1pr\ i_{N_{pr}}{}^1]\ |^2N^2|$ $|^2V_4{}^2|^1)^1|.$

Special type   The people *wanted him to be governor.*

$|^1m\ N^1|$ $|^1V_4{}^1|$ $|^1|^2N^2|$ $|^2“to”\ V_1{}^2|$ $|^2N^2|^1|.$

5. *The Predicate Structure*

The formula consists of the formulas of nuclear sentence A 1, A 2, A 3 and C without the S. Also (and almost exclusively in writing) it consists of a V_1 form, usually with *to,* or a V_3 form followed by an O_2 or O_1O_2 or O_2C or C.

Example:

He intended *to kill the old ladies.*

$|^1N_p{}^1|$ $|^1V_4{}^1|$ $|^1|^2“to”\ V_1{}^2|$ $|^2m\ M\ N^2|^1|.$

Notice that the segments of the predicate structure are marked like a nuclear sentence. This is done to emphasize the likeness between the two.

6. *The Coordination Structure*

The formula simply requires that the coordinator be put in the appropriate place between the items connected. It is important that when a coordination structure consists of more than two items a comma be placed wherever a c has been omitted. Slant lines must always be used to mark the boundaries of the structure.

Examples: Men and women

$/^1N\ c\ N^1/$

in the house and in the garage

$/^1\ pr\ m\ N_{pr}\ c\ pr\ m\ N_{pr}{}^1/$

men, women and children

$/^1N,\ N\ c\ N^1/$

D. OTHER SYMBOLS

S   means "subject" when nuclear sentences are being discussed

S   means "sentence" in other contexts

T   means "transformation"

E. SUMMARY OF RELATION SIGNALS

1. Parts of nuclear sentences are separated by numbered vertical lines.

2. Modifiers of particular words are enclosed in numbered parentheses with an arrow pointing to the modified words: ← (M). Single-word modifiers usually do not need a relation-signal unless there are two words that might be modified. Then an arrow is drawn to point to the proper word.

   Examples: "A very old house" as contrasted to "An old white house." The former would be m M → M N, the latter m M M N.

3. Sentence modifiers are enclosed in numbered square brackets: [¹ ¹].

4. Coordination structures are enclosed in numbered slant lines: /¹ ¹/.

5. Interrupted structures mark the beginning and end of the interruption by appropriate broken lines. The commonest examples occur in included nuclear sentences and in multi-word verbs, i.e.,: "has certainly been decided":

   |¹v| M |v V₅¹|.

6. The symbol ⟶≫ means "is to be expressed as."

7. Individual words (these are written out with quotation marks around them):

   Question Signallers — "do," "does," "did"

   Negators — "not," "never"

   Passive Transformation Signallers — "be," "get," "by"

   V₁ Signaller — "to"

Punctuation

As we have seen (p. 19), the marks of punctuation in written English are symbols for the supra-segmental phonemes of speech. Thus the period and question mark and exclamation point are symbols for "end of sentence" (# and ||), the comma and dash are symbols for the sound phenomena associated with the juncture-marker | and the semicolon is a substitute for the coordinators. Unfortunately no generally accepted system of using these symbols has been worked out for written English. At most one can only offer a system that will be helpful and unobtrusive, without claiming that it is the best or the only "correct" system. The following statements do this, and consequently cannot hope to be acceptable to everyone who is expert in the use of the written language.

Period and question mark

The period and the question mark are generally acceptable as symbols for the ends of sentences and, with the exclamation point, are normally the only three symbols used for this purpose. But the period is used for other purposes also, and the question mark is often superfluous.

The end of a sentence is always marked by a period unless the sentence is a question transformation on an exclamation. It is a symbol for #, and any reader will automatically think of the sound pattern of # when he sees a period. In written English the period almost always marks the end of a nuclear sentence, though of course there are some exceptions, possibly averaging one or two per hundred sentences.

The period is also used conventionally to identify an abbreviation that has become acceptable in writing, such as Mr., Dr., Mass., N. Y., Ph.D. and so on. However, with the exception of the designations of a person's status (Mr., Mrs., Dr., Ph.D.) it is preferable not to use abbreviations in writing. It is to be noted that *Miss* is not considered an abbreviation, though in fact it is.

Three periods in succession are used to mark omissions from quoted material. For example, if the sentence above, "The period is also used conventionally to identify an abbreviation in writing, such as Mr., Dr., Mass., N. Y., Ph.D. and so on," were quoted with omissions it would appear like this: "The period is also used . . . to identify an abbreviation. . . ."

The question mark is used at the ends of questions. But it is necessary only when there is no other signal for the question transformation. Such a sentence as *You want to go?* has the form of a nuclear sentence, and without the ? would end with #. But the question mark indicates that || is to occur at the end. Except for this particular type of question, however, the question mark is not needed. If a sentence starts with a form of *be* or with any other auxiliary verb or with an interrogator, there is no need for the question mark, and no native English speaker would interpret a sentence starting in this fashion as anything but a question—unless of course some later signal cancels the question signal.

In the following examples are illustrated the various question signals and the ways in which they are sometimes cancelled:

Where have you been?
Where you have been is no concern of mine.
(The cancellation is made by the S preceding the auxiliary verb instead of following it as in the first sentence.)
Did you ask me a question?
Have you ever seen a cameleopard?
Was he the one you meant?
What did you do?
What you did is not important.
(As in the sentence above beginning with *where*, the cancellation is made by the S following *what*.)

Who came with you?
What happened?
What happened was surprising indeed.
(The cancellation is caused by our recognition that *what hap-pened* is an included nuclear sentence which is the S of *was surprising indeed*.)

Except in sentences where the form is that of a nuclear sentence, the question mark is therefore superflous. And in those questions having the form of nuclear sentences, the question mark could be more helpful if it occurred at the beginning rather than at the end of the sentence.

The exclamation point

The exclamation point not only marks the end of the sentence; it also informs the reader about the sorts of supra-segmental phonemes to be used. As an end-of-sentence marker it means #. If the sentence is to end with || a question mark would be used, whatever the supra-segmental phonemes. In the sentence *What a fool I had been!*, the main difference from the normal is the greater relative stress on the word *fool*. The normal stress markings would be: what a fool I had been; the exclamation point makes it: what a fool I had been. But of course the exclamation point may be ambiguous in its directions. The sentence *He actually walked ten miles!* could have its principal stress on *actually*, on *walked* or on *miles*, or even perhaps on *he*. The exclamation point doesn't indicate which is to be chosen. As a result we can only say about the exclamation point that it directs the reader to make a departure from the normal stress pattern; it does not describe exactly what the difference should be. Only the context or the feeling of the reader can decide this. The exclamation point would also be more useful if it preceded the sentence rather than followed it.

The semicolon

The semicolon is best thought of as a substitute for one of the coordinators (see p. 98). That is, it is placed between two or more

non-included nuclear sentences, to suggest a closer relationship between them than would be suggested by a period. On the whole a
coordinator is to be preferred to a semicolon, since it indicates something about the relationship, but when the relationship is not clearly
one that can be expressed by a coordinator, or when the writer
prefers to leave the relationship unstated, the semicolon is a legitimate
device to use. The following sentences show various acceptable uses
of the semicolon.

> The shortstop was the best hitter on the team; in fact, he was
> leading the league at the time.
> (Here no coordinator can easily be substituted.)
> Many men cannot cope with machines; I am one of them.
> (*And* could be used, but it seems inadequate here.)
> The process is very difficult to follow; to do so requires a con-
> siderable knowledge of mathematics.
> (Here *for* could be an appropriate coordinator, and the decision
> to use the semicolon is arbitrary and perhaps whimsical on the
> part of the writer.)

The semicolon, then, has only one essential use in written English,
i.e., to serve as a coordinator-substitute between non-included nuclear
sentences. No other use need be learned, though many writers do, in
fact, use it in other situations.

The comma

The preceding marks of punctuation are relatively simple in their
use. The comma is not. While it is associated with the juncture
marked |, the association is neither clear nor regular, and the use of
commas by different professional writers varies widely. The only
generalization that can be made is that the more apparent the | junc-
ture the more likely it is that a comma will be used. In modern writing
far fewer commas are used than in writing two hundred or even one
hundred years ago. Thus most of the "rules" given in conventional
handbooks do not apply to much modern writing, since they are
based on rather old-fashioned practices. Possibly the increase in reading speed has enabled modern readers to see larger segments of a line

of print and thus to anticipate and prepare for junctures without the constant aid of punctuation signals. Then too, modern sentences tend to be shorter than sentences written in former times; consequently they tend to have fewer junctures.

The remark made above is, therefore, more applicable to commas than to other marks of punctuation, i.e., there is little agreement in the practices of professional writers about the use of commas. In general American writers seem to use more commas than do English writers, but this is by no means always true. Any generalizations made about the use of commas simply cannot be called rules. They are suggestions for a system that will not be conspicuously odd and that will probably not bother anyone. The statements below should be taken in this spirit, and departures from them should not necessarily be considered mistakes.

Commas to prevent misreading.

(1) The most important use for commas is to identify a | juncture when a reader might not be aware of it until later in the sentence. If his awareness comes too late it may require him to reread the sentence and thus interfere with his easy comprehension of what is being said. Such a sentence as *He wanted assurances and promises for my future conduct would not satisfy him* illustrates such a situation. The two nouns *assurances* and *promises* appear to be connected by the coordinator *and*. But five words later in the sentence it becomes clear that the *and connects* two nuclear sentences, not two nouns. Thus a | juncture must occur before *and*. If this juncture is marked with a comma, the reader is warned to think of a juncture at this point and thus the reader does not become confused. It is rather common for a nuclear sentence both to end with a noun and to begin with a noun; consequently the situation illustrated above is fairly frequent. Thus the practice has grown up of putting a comma in front of all coordinators that join non-included nuclear sentences. This then is our first generalization: COMMAS SHOULD BE PLACED BEFORE ALL COORDINATORS THAT CONNECT NON-INCLUDED NUCLEAR SENTENCES OR TRANSFORMATIONS OF NON-INCLUDED NUCLEAR SENTENCES. It must be repeated that not all professionals do this regularly, as a little investigation of a contemporary piece of writing will show, but if one does what the generalization says, he will never go wrong. There seems to be a

tendency to put commas more regularly before *but* than before the other coordinators. It seems reasonable therefore to depart from this generalization less frequently when the coordinator is *but*.

(2) Another | juncture that is frequently not recognized without a comma occurs after a sentence modifier at the beginning of a nuclear sentence. This happens because such sentence modifiers often end with (a) verb forms which may be followed by an O_2, (b) words that can appear as modifiers or (c) words that can appear as prepositions. If the S of the following nuclear sentence is not preceded by a noun marker in the case of (b) there is a tendency to relate the modifier with the following noun. In the situation named in (a) and (c) even a noun marker will not signal the juncture. Some examples are:

Because the problem was *confusing scientists* were engaged to work on it. (a)
While father *was considering the whole situation* changed. (a)
In *performing plays* often are distorted. (a)
Since it was *spring weather* predictions were uncertain. (b)
When the outlook was *good news* was broadcast frequently. (b)
When John received *his tickets* to the opera were almost unobtainable. (b)
When the ball was *over his head* was swimming. (c)
While the plane was passing *over the men* remained absolutely still. (c)
A short time *after the events* began to take shape in his mind. (c)

In reading the sentences without punctuation anyone is likely to mistake the relationship among the italicized words because he fails to identify the juncture after the first italicized word. If this happens, the reader must reread the sentence and thus unnecessarily delay his progress through the discourse. Naturally not all sentences with such a situation are confusing. In the sentences that follow, either some signal or the impossibility of the meaning makes the juncture recognizable at once.

After *pausing the little girl went up the street.*
When the weather is *good grass seeds* come up quickly.

When the shower was *over a rainbow* appeared.
If the fog *increases the ship* must slow down.
Because the plan was *successful the rewards* were great.
In acting for the *best the parents* often do great harm.
While they were very *handsome the buildings* were not well
maintained.

The first four sentences above cannot be misread because of the impossibility of the second italicized word being in the relation of object to or of being modified by the first word. The last three signal the juncture by having a marker between the potential modifier and the word to be modified. As we have previously seen, single-word modifiers of nouns almost never come outside the marker, except in special situations (see pages 188–190).

Our second generalization will be: A SENTENCE MODIFIER AT THE BEGINNING OF A SENTENCE SHOULD BE FOLLOWED BY A COMMA IF A MISTAKEN RELATIONSHIP BETWEEN THE LAST WORD OF THE MODIFIER AND THE FIRST WORD OF THE FOLLOWING STRUCTURE IS POSSIBLE. If there is the slightest possibility of the reader's being misled the comma should be inserted. Many professional writers are rather careless about this.

If the sentence modifier is a single word like *therefore, thus, so* or a conventionalized prepositional phrase like *in fact, of course,* the comma is seldom necessary, since words and structures of this kind seldom have a potential relationship with the first word of the following structure.

The two situations described above produce most of the confusion that comes from failing to recognize a very important juncture. However, such potential misreadings may occur at any place in a sentence where a possible relationship between words turns out to be a false relationship. Some examples are:

He came *to the water* being very cold.
The police were still *pursuing the fugitives* having given signs of weakening.
There was no one *ready to tell the truth*.
For this course seniors are the *best students* being what they are.

We may make a third generalization, which includes the first two. WHENEVER THE ORDER OF WORDS MAKES POSSIBLE A MISTAKEN RELATION-SHIP BETWEEN A VERB AND AN OBJECT, A MODIFIER AND A MODIFI-ABLE WORD OR A PREPOSITION AND A FOLLOWING NOUN, A COMMA BETWEEN THE TWO ELEMENTS INVOLVED WILL INSURE RECOGNITION OF THE NECESSARY JUNCTURE.

Other comma uses

(1) A series of words or structures forming a coordination structure may be written as follows:

My father was tall and broad and handsome.

It may also be written:

My father was tall, broad and handsome.

In such a series the comma substitutes for a coordinator. For many years there has been a difference of practice in punctuating such a series. Many people use the punctuation given above, which seems logical enough if we think of the comma as a coordinator-substitute. But perhaps equally popular is the practice of putting an additional comma before the *and*. This perhaps is illogical, but it happens. There is, therefore, no reason to change your habits if you are in the practice of putting a comma before *and*. However it is desirable to be consistent and to use the same method regularly. The generalization is: IN A COORDINATION STRUCTURE A COMMA SHOULD BE SUBSTITUTED FOR EVERY OMITTED COORDINATOR, UNLESS THE CO-ORDINATED STRUCTURES ARE NON-INCLUDED NUCLEAR SENTENCES. (See page 122.)

(2) A useful distinction between two types of included nuclear sentences is made by using commas. Included nuclear sentences which modify nouns or noun substitutes are of two kinds. They are distinguished by the prominence of the juncture between the noun modified and the includer. The sentence *My brother who lives in Wichita is a broker* may be said with a relatively inconspicuous juncture after *brother,* or with a relatively conspicuous juncture. The meaning of the total sentence is different as a result of this. If an inconspicuous

juncture is used a hearer will assume that the included nuclear sentence identifies one particular brother out of two or more brothers. If the conspicuous juncture is used the hearer will assume that the speaker has only one brother. This difference in conspicuousness of juncture is indicated in writing by putting a comma before *who* when a conspicuous juncture would be used in speech. The included sentence with the conspicuous juncture is often called "non-restrictive," the one with the inconspicuous juncture is called "restrictive."

When writing such sentences one should (indeed, must) be aware of the prominence of the juncture which he wants the reader to recognize and insert a comma when he wants the reader to recognize a conspicuous juncture. The following sentences (written without commas) should be read aloud. Decide on the basis of the juncture you hear just before the includer whether or not they should have punctuation. (Some of them can be read in two ways.)

The Civil Rights bill which has been holding up legislation in Congress is likely to be passed soon.

My very best—indeed my only—real friend whom I've known since we were in primary school has just been elected mayor.

That little fellow who's sitting on the curb is my nephew.

The Declaration of Independence which was proclaimed in 1776 was written by Thomas Jefferson.

Young men who chase girls have more fun than young men who don't.

This young man who has been in my composition class is already deeply involved with a blonde from Texas.

A great deal of trouble which could easily have been avoided came from his brashness.

The lovely dark-haired girl that he was watching seemed to be enjoying herself greatly.

One thing should be noticed, i.e., when the includer is *that,* there will never be a conspicuous juncture before it.

The generalization is: A CONSPICUOUS JUNCTURE BEFORE AN INCLUDED NUCLEAR SENTENCE MODIFYING A NOUN OR A NOUN SUBSTITUTE SHOULD BE SIGNALLED BY PUTTING A COMMA IN FRONT OF THE INCLUDER.

(3) All other uses of the comma are largely a matter of taste, and no really successful generalizations can be made. It is probably true to say that the more conspicuous a juncture is, the more likely a comma will be used to mark it, but apparently people differ in their judgment as to *how* conspicuous a juncture must be to justify a comma. If the generalizations given above are followed consistently, however, few problems will arise and you may trust your own judgment for deciding when to use additional commas.

Other punctuation marks

One can get along perfectly well in most writing with the five marks of punctuation discussed so far. But other marks of punctuation do exist and you may want to try them out.

The most important are dashes, parentheses and brackets. Dashes and parentheses are used like commas—to indicate conspicuous junctures, particularly when these junctures occur at the beginning and/or end of a fairly elaborate syntax structure that interrupts an already started structure. Dashes are generally used more frequently in informal writing, parentheses in more formal writing. Some examples are:

> She put on a raincoat—it was a cloudy day—before going to shop.
> The most important plays of Shakespeare (those written between 1598 and 1610) are the ones most often produced nowadays.
> Not many people would have thought—circumstances being as they are—that such a project could possibly succeed.
> The most important political problem (I speak of course of national problems) is that of integration.

None of the uses illustrated above are necessary, since the ideas could be conveyed by slight structural changes, i.e.,

> Since it was a cloudy day she put on a raincoat before going to shop.
> The most important plays of Shakespeare, those written between

1598 and 1610, are the ones most frequently produced nowadays.

Circumstances being as they are, not many people would have
thought that such a project could possibly succeed.

The most important political problem that concerns the whole
nation is that of integration.

It is probably best to limit the use of these two marks of punctuation and to rely mainly on commas.

Brackets have a special use and should be confined to this use.
When a quotation appears in a piece of writing brackets are used to
show that a certain word or group of words did not appear in the
original quotation but were supplied by the quoter to insure clarity.
For example, suppose you wish to quote the following passage and
you have not previously mentioned the name of the man for whom
"he" stands. "He was the creator of the single-tax system." You would
do it this way "[Henry George] was the creator of the single-tax
system." This is the only situation in which brackets are necessary.

A fourth additional mark of punctuation is the colon. This is
normally used after the salutation in letters, i.e., "Dear George:"
"Dear Doctor Jones:" and so on. Both in informal and formal letters,
this is the current practice.

Quotation marks may also be considered as punctuation, though
they do not always have something to do with supra-segmental
phonemes. Their uses may be summed up as follows:

(1) Quotation marks are used around all quoted material that
is a part of the text, whether its source is oral or written. (And note
that periods and commas *always* precede closing quotation marks.
This is purely a convention, but it is consistently followed.)

(2) When quotations contain other quotations such as "He said,
'I don't want to go,'" single quotes are used around the inner quotation.

(3) When a typewriten passage more than three or four lines long
is quoted, it is set off from the text by being indented further on
both sides and, if the text is double-spaced, by being single-spaced.
Quotation marks are *not* used, unless of course there is some inner
quotation.

(4) Quotation marks may be used when you are speaking of a word as a word or as a grammatical unit.

(5) Quotation marks are used to suggest that the writer is using a word ironically or in a special meaning that the context should make clear.

(6) Quotation marks are often used the first time a technical term is used, especially when a definition precedes or follows.